4/24

Antique
Arms and Armour

Antique
Arms and Armour

Frederick Wilkinson

Ward Lock Ltd London

Acknowledgments

Many people have helped in differing ways to produce this book; dealers and collectors have given information and auctioneers have given me the freedom of their photographic records. To all these and to other friends I sincerely express my gratitude and debt; my special thanks must go to Ron Dufty, Doug Nie and L. Rawlins of Weller and Dufty, T. Elliot of Elliot and Snowdon and David Jeffcoat of Sotheby & Co.

© Frederick Wilkinson 1972
ISBN 0 7063 1024 1

First published in Great Britain 1972
by Ward Lock Limited, 116 Baker Street, London, W1M 2BB

Printed and bound by Editorial Fher SA, Bilbao, Spain.

Dedication to M.N.S.

The Photographs

The photographs have been chosen with the idea of showing as wide a range of items as possible, some quite common, some very rare. Most have come from various auction rooms and again this was a deliberate choice, since it is from such sales that many of the items offered by dealers originate. Other pieces shown are from private collections and none from the major national collections has been included for the main emphasis has been on the items that a collector, with luck and capital, might reasonably hope to acquire.

The author and publishers wish to thank the following for their kind permission to reproduce photographs:

R. Amos   S.W.35, 43; B.4, 5, 8.

J. Angolia   S.W.45.

H. L. Blackmore   G.43; S.W.1.

Collectors Arms Antiques   G.75; E.D.8, 12.

A. Dove   O.S.2.

S. Durrant   G.18, 25.

Elliot and Snowden. G. 2, 9, 21, 24, 27, 47, 57, 60, 63; S.W. 36, 42; E.D. 7; O.S. 6, 7, 8; A. 15, 20, 21, 22, 23, 24; O.A. 6, 7, 8.

D. S. H. Gyngell   G.26; A.16; S.W.7.

G. Kellam   E.D.13.

G. Mungeam   S.W.8, 8a, 9, 13, 17; E.D.4, 5; A.18, 19; P.A.3.

Penrose Collection   O.S.4.

Sotheby & Co. G. 3, 4, 5, 5A, 6, 7, 10, 11, 12, 12A, 15, 23, 30, 32, 32A, 35, 36, 37, 38, 39, 40, 41, 41A, 46, 47, 47A, 47B, 48, 51, 56, 58, 59, 61, 62, 64, 65, 66, 67, 68, 70, 72, 77A, 78, 79, 80, 81; S.W. 3, 4, 5, 10, 11, 12, 15, 16, 18, 20, 21, 23, 25, 26, 27, 40, 46, 46A; E.D. 1, 2, 3, 9, 10; O.S. 4, 5; A. 1, 2, 3, 4, 5, 6, 7, 8, 9, 10, 11, 12, 13; O.A. 1, 2, 3; P.A. 1, 2.

D. Spalding   S.W.29, 30.

F. Stephens   S.W.44, 47; E.D.14, 15.

Weller and Dufty. G. 14, 16, 17, 22, 50, 52, 53, 54, 55, 71, 74, 75, 76, 77; S.W. 22, 31, 32, 33, 38, 39; E.D. 6, 11; O.D. 1, 2; O.S. 1, 5, 9; A. 14, 17; O.A. 4, 5.

Contents

Introduction

In the intervening period since the publication of SMALL ARMS (1965) and SWORDS AND DAGGERS (1967) changes have occurred in the field of arms and armour. One of the most evident has been the marked growth of interest both in the collecting and the study of weapons and armour of all types. This continuing interest owes its growth to a number of factors, some of which are general whilst others are peculiar to this field.

This developing interest has had two main effects; obviously the law of supply and demand has applied and the increased number of collectors chasing a limited number of specimens has had the inevitable result of pushing up prices. One result of higher prices has been to encourage collectors to be more adventurous and to explore new fields. Barred from acquiring certain weapons which have become too expensive, many have turned to less conventional arms and to items previously rather scorned. For many years pistols held pride of place but as these appreciated in value some collectors turned to edged weapons and armour. Greater interest in these areas had exactly the same effect and an increased demand which, in turn, led collectors to dabble in items such as military head-dresses, uniforms and badges. Interest in previously neglected fields such as Asiatic weapons was also aroused but in each and every case the greater demand resulted in an upward swing of prices.

The second effect of the increased interest was a demand for authoritative and reliable books identifying and describing the many varieties of weapons and armour. Publishers were naturally only too ready to meet this need and books, both general and specific, dealing with various topics in this field made their appearance—today the flood of new books continues unabated. In addition to new books based on original research a number of facsimile reprints of some of the earlier, and previously scarce, books have appeared. Increased knowledge and easier availability of knowledge naturally evoked further interest in the subject.

Some of this increased interest has been purely academic but in many cases the greater knowledge encouraged more collectors and consequently pushed prices up even more.

There has also been the increased interest by investor buyers of arms and armour; such individuals see the items simply as a basic trading commodity which must, if the past trend continues, appreciate in value. Their prime consideration is to buy only pieces which will show the greatest increase. The effect on the market has been to push up the prices of many good quality pieces proportionally higher than for ordinary items.

Some of the factors which have stimulated interest are not peculiar to arms and armour for the collecting of all antiques has become very popular. There is no question that for many people there has been a revulsion, albeit a romantic one, against the anonymity and standardisation of modern living. This has expressed itself in an increased demand for antiques which reflect an individuality, a quality of uniqueness, which seems to be lacking in present day life.

Is it then no longer feasible, desirable or even possible for the smaller collector to build up a collection? Happily the general answer must be no. Certainly there are some fields where only the wealthiest collectors can hope to acquire specimens; wheel-lock pistols, complete armours and individual pieces of rarity and quality may be counted amongst such items. Even with the greatly increased demand from collectors and dealers the possibility of building up a reasonable collection which must inevitably appreciate in value, is sufficiently strong to encourage a collector. Certainly one will find that it is not so easy to acquire good quality specimens or even the most ordinary items but the possibility of turning up a 'sleeper', a hitherto undiscovered treasure, is still there and there have been a number of examples of this happy state of affairs during the past few years.

Quite apart from the pleasure of possession the study and collecting of arms and armour offers a field of immense opportunity for original research, romantic interests and even profitable involvement. Whatever the motivation, be it pleasure or profit, the return will be enhanced by a sound knowledge of the subject. Indeed knowledge has become more essential than ever for 'bad buys' are becoming too expensive to afford.

It is hoped that in the following chapters the reader will find some guidance and information which will help him to explore and enjoy the fascinating study of arms and armour.

The Story of the Gun

Missile weapons are probably as old as man, the long bow was certainly in use during the Neolithic period and the bow and the sling were to remain the standard missile weapons for many thousands of years. Their supremacy in battle was not challenged until the 11th century when some unknown Chinese with a sense of curiosity and some intuition, mixed together three chemicals, sulphur, saltpetre and charcoal. When this mixture was ignited it produced a loud roar, a flash and a cloud of smoke worthy of the fieriest of Chinese dragons. For a century or so this strange mixture appears to have been limited to frightening and confusing an enemy but evidence suggests that during the 13th century another Chinese inventor produced a new weapon. He found that if this strange mixture was compressed within a bamboo tube and some small projectile placed over the charge, the combined effect of flame, smoke and flash was to eject the projectile with considerable force over some distance. This then was the beginning of the gun, a weapon which was to change the entire concept of warfare throughout the world.

Knowledge of this unusual and frightening compound spread slowly across the continent of Asia and then, possibly via India and North Africa, it eventually reached Europe in the 13th century. The precise date of its arrival is uncertain but a case has been made out to show that there is an anagram of its formula contained within the work of Roger Bacon. The case is by no means irrefutable but it would seem likely that Europe had knowledge of the formula of gunpowder by the mid 13th century. The first use of gunpowder as a propellant for missiles is usually taken to be the early 14th century for there are two contemporary documents of identical date, 1326, which indicate clearly that guns were in existence at this time. The town records of Florence show the appointment of men to manufacture ammunition for cannon required to defend the state. The English evidence takes the form of small, but highly detailed sketches contained within the margins of two documents written by Walter de Milemete. Both show mailed knights igniting gunpowder contained in pot-shaped containers from which project the end of an arrow. Confirmatory evidence of the accuracy of the illustrations is to be found in a surviving specimen of a small hand-gun found at Loshult in Sweden. In basic form this bronze gun closely resembles that shown on the Milemete manuscript. Generally speaking the earliest firearms appear to have been artillery widely advocated for use in demolishing the strong castle walls then in use.

Once the concept of projecting a missile had evolved it was not long before smaller versions of the cannon were being produced and these hand-guns became more and more common. They consisted essentially of a miniature cannon fastened to a wooden or metal bar, the 'stock'. The vast majority were muzzle loading which means that powder and ball were loaded in through the muzzle and rammed home into the breech at the rear of the barrel. At right angles to the breech a small hole was drilled through the wall of the barrel and this touchhole allowed direct access to the charge of powder. It is by no means certain what form the first ignition systems took; the knights in the Milemete manuscript appear to be using some form of heated wire although it may well be that the shape represents a pair of tongs with which the firer grasped a piece of glowing ember or smouldering moss. Whatever the actual method the glowing end was applied to the touchhole igniting the powder to create the explosion which ejected the missile.

Early hand-guns were almost certainly inaccurate for, quite apart from the variations of trajectory caused by differences in charges and bullets, there was no means of sighting so that aiming was largely a matter of guess-work and instinct. An improvement in design appeared, probably during the early 15th century, when a simple mechanical means of applying ignition was fitted to the firearm. This took the form of a Z shaped bar attached to the side of the stock and pivoted at the centre; into the top arm of the Z was fitted a piece of match, cord soaked in saltpetre. Pressure on the lower section of the Z caused the upper section to swing forward and the glowing end of the match was pressed down directly into the touchhole to ignite the charge. When pressure was removed from the lower half of the serpentine a simple spring arrangement caused the arm to rise up clear of the touchhole.

The early stock, or wooden body of the gun had originally been a solid length of wood designed merely to hold the barrel securely and safely but gradually a butt evolved and this was a simple, but highly important development for it was now possible for the soldier to aim the muzzle of his weapon at a specific target. By the late 15th century the general shape of the musket—a name derived from *moschetto* (Italian for hawk), had taken on its more or less traditional shape. The simple serpentine had been replaced by a slightly more complex system of levers, springs and sears although the basic system of operation remained the same. Early muskets were made with a heavy, four feet long barrel which was so weighty that it was difficult for the average soldier to support and aim the weapon with any degree of steadiness. To overcome this problem a simple wooden support, with a U-shaped metal arm affixed to the top, the 'rest', was introduced to enable the musketeer to steady the weapon when firing. Smaller versions of the musket, known as 'carbines', were also introduced during the 16th and 17th centuries.

The ease of manufacture and low cost of production encouraged the adoption of this weapon by the armies of Europe but the one great disadvantage of the firearm compared with other missile arms was that once the musketeer had discharged a shot his empty weapon was more or less useless, cumbersome and certainly extremely inconvenient.

Loading a musket involved a complicated sequence of movements and although the authors of drill books vary their details the basic routine was standard. After firing a shot the match was removed from the serpentine and, together with the loose end which was also alight as a reserve means of ignition, was held between the fingers of the left hand. From a horn container a measured charge of powder was poured down the barrel of the musket whilst from another pocket or bag the musketeer extracted a cast lead ball, often wrapped in a greased patch. Housed in the wooden stock beneath the barrel was a long wooden rod, sometimes tipped with iron, and this ramrod was withdrawn from its housing and used to hammer down the ball so that it sat securely on the powder in the breech; it was then replaced. Next a small pan fitted at the side of the barrel adjacent to the touch hole was filled with some fine grained powder from a second powder container. In order to prevent this priming powder being blown away or tipped off, it was covered by a small pivoted plate. One end of the match was replaced in the serpentine and the weapon was at last ready to fire once the pan cover was swung clear and the trigger pressed.

Heavy matchlock muskets were to remain the commonest military firearm for many years until they were gradually replaced by newer weapons, a process which started around the middle of the 17th century.

The cheapness and ease of construction of the matchlock musket and carbine were important factors in ensuring that it was adopted and used for long periods by the majority of European armies. Another great virtue was the fact that its use required little basic training; once the routine tasks of loading and firing had been mastered, the main necessity in battle was to ensure that the musketeers were there in numbers and able to maintain a reasonable rate of fire. However there were certain inherent disadvantages in the matchlock system. Matchlock muskets had to be prepared well in advance of any possible action since it was essential that the match be well alight. As a result it could well be burning for extended periods so that considerable stocks had to be held in reserve and carried along with the troops. The musketeer was very much at the mercy of weather which could extinguish his match and although ingenious devices were introduced to protect it from wind and rain these were constant hazards for the musketeer. At night it was impossible to move groups of musketeers in secrecy for the glowing ends of the match must betray their presence. The exposed glowing match was a constant source of danger since in any battle there was certain to be quantities of powder lying about and accidents were by no means uncommon. The problems involved in handling a length of glowing match whilst riding a horse were considerable and although a few matchlock pistols were produced, particularly in India, they were never common. These serious disadvantages more than counterbalanced the simplicity of manufacture and the low cost of the matchlock and soon an alternative method of ignition was at hand.

This had first been experimented with early in the 16th century and whereas the matchlock required a piece of glowing match the alternative system had the tremendous virtue of producing fire only when required. Leonardo da Vinci certainly toyed with the idea even if he was not the inventor for simple sketches among his prodigious output illustrate a perfectly workable device using this new system. To ignite the powder, sparks were produced by means of friction between pieces of certain minerals and a steel wheel. It was found that iron pyrites, occurring over large areas of Europe, was the most practical mineral available. A piece was gripped between the vice-like jaws of the pivoted arm known as the 'dogs-head'. When lowered into position this dogs-head pressed the pyrites against the circumference of a steel wheel into which had been cut a series of grooves and notches. To prepare the mechanism the wheel was rotated by means of a key and, by way of a small chain and a heavy V spring, was placed under tension and locked into position by an arm, the 'sear', which engaged with a small recess on the side of the wheel. If the sear were now withdrawn from its locked position the wheel, activated by the spring, was forced to rotate quickly. Friction between the pyrites and steel produced a stream of sparks which, falling into the gunpowder in the pan, ignited it in exactly the same way as a burning match. This system, which was known as the wheel-lock, was to remain in use on certain weapons well on towards the end of the 17th century.

The wheel-lock mechanism had several very real virtues, chief of which was its instant availability for a weapon could now be loaded, the lock spanned, that is wound up, placed to one side and left for any length of time. It could be picked up and on pressing the trigger the charge was ignited without any further attention or preparation. Since the mechanism could be constructed in any size, limited only by the skill of the maker, as might be expected a large variety of guns were produced with this system of ignition ranging from large wall pieces to very delicate and graceful pistols, probably so named after the Italian town of Pistoia.

However efficient and reliable the wheel-lock mechanism might be it did suffer from some serious drawbacks. The mechanism itself was complex and quite difficult to manufacture and consequently it was liable to jamming and breaking and, of course, its cost was very high. Wheel-lock weapons were generally so expensive that their issue was limited to select bodyguards and some cavalry units. This latter development was to have a profound effect on the history of warfare for, for the first time, bodies of lightly armoured, quick moving troops could attack with firearms.

Complexity and high cost were factors which seriously limited the production of the wheel-lock and gunmakers were under some commercial and political pressure to perfect a cheaper method of mechanical ignition. The wheel-lock had demonstrated very clearly the great advantage of mechanical ignition over the older system using combustion and the gunmakers searched for an alternative mechanical system. During the early 16th century a simple mechanism, now designated the Baltic lock, was recorded in Scandinavia and areas bordering the Baltic sea. A long, pivoted arm terminated in adjustable jaws which held a piece of flint and, impelled by a spring, this arm and the flint were swung down and forward to rub along the flat surface of a piece of steel situated just above the pan. Friction between steel and flint produced small, incandescent sparks which fell into the priming powder to ignite the main charge of powder. This basic flintlock mechanism, simple and reliable, was to undergo modifications and developments but for the next three hundred years it was to remain the main means of firearm ignition.

Surviving Baltic locks are, generally speaking, fairly crude but further south in Italy and Germany, more sophisticated forms of the mechanism were produced. This type of lock is usually known to collectors as a 'snaphaunce'. The basic principle was the same in that the 'cock', or arm, still grasped the piece of flint which struck against the steel plate; whilst the priming powder was still protected

15

by a sliding, or pivoted cover and it was necessary to remove the pan cover before firing. Sometimes this pan cover was removed manually, but on other weapons it was linked to the cock by levers so that the pan was automatically uncovered as the cock swung forward.

The snaphaunce mechanism had the virtue of simplicity of construction and by its very nature it incorporated a safety device for if the pivoted arm to which was secured the steel, was swung clear of the pan then it was impossible for sparks to be struck and the weapon could not be fired. Under normal circumstances the pivoted arm was pushed forward clear of the pan by the impetus of the flint but, as early as the 1580s some gunsmiths were combining the pan cover and steel into a single L shaped piece, usually known as the 'frizzen', although this system did not become generally adopted until the mid 17th century. The virtue of this combination was that the mechanism was simplified since the pan cover, now an integral part of the steel, was automatically opened at the instant that the sparks were struck; the action was simple, reliable and precise. On most of the early snaphaunce pistols the mainspring, a heavy V shaped one, was mounted on the outside of the lock plate and the cock was so placed that the tip of it pressed on one end of the spring. As the cock was pulled back the spring was compressed and when fully retracted a small metal arm, the sear, projected through a small hole in the lockplate and held the cock in place. Pressure on the trigger retracted the sear and allowed the cock, impelled by the spring, to swing forward and strike sparks. A few snaphaunces, probably of German manufacture, differed in that the mainspring was internally mounted but this practice did not gain general acceptance for some time.

Early in the 17th century, probably during the first decade, a provincial French gunmaker—Marin le Bourgeoys, introduced a new design of lock, usually referred to as the French lock and which became standard for the next two hundred and fifty years. The French lock had an L shaped frizzen but its main distinction was in the design of the internal mechanism. The cock holding the flint was secured to a square cut shank projecting from a shaped block sitting on the inside of the lock plate. This block, known as the 'tumbler', had two slots one deeper than the other. The trigger operated a small L shaped bar, the sear, the edge of which pressed against the rim of the tumbler; as the cock was pulled back the sear rode over the face of the tumbler until it clicked [it was under spring pressure] into the first slot. This was so shaped that pressure on the trigger could not disengage the sear from this first slot. Since the cock had made only part of the rotation necessary before it could fire this position was known as 'half cock' and served as a good safety locking device enabling the user to carry the flintlock, fully loaded and primed, with a reasonable degree of safety against accidental discharge. In order to activate the lock the cock had to be pulled back further and this movement disengaged the sear from the first slot and allowed it to ride over the face of the tumbler to engage with the second, shallower and slightly angled cut. Pressure on the trigger could disengage the sear from the tumbler so that the cock, impelled by a large V shaped spring bearing on the tumbler, swung forward through an arc allowing the flint to rub down the face of the frizzen and produce the requisite sparks. This French lock was adopted by most gunmakers with the exception of some based around the Mediterranean and these produced a characteristic style of lock usually designated as a 'miquelet'. From around 1650 until 1830 the French lock was the standard type of lock found in the great majority of firearms, pistols and long arms. There were changes in detail and attempts to improve efficiency but the basic design remained the same.

The flintlock was reliable, cheap and generally efficient. The piece of flint was reckoned to be good for some thirty shots before it required changing although, of course, this was an average figure and in some cases the flint was worn out much sooner whilst a good quality piece might well serve for considerably more than thirty shots. Although the mechanism was efficient a number of misfires did occur. For a variety of reasons the striking flint might not produce enough sparks or wind could divert the sparks or perhaps rain prevented their formation, but the net result was the same, the gun did not fire. A second and, for the hunter, more serious disadvantage was the hangfire. When the trigger was pressed a sequence of events followed; the sear was removed, the cock swung forward striking the frizzen, the flint scraped down the face of the frizzen pushing it clear so that the sparks fell into the priming pan, the priming flashed and the flame passed through the touchhole into the breech of the weapon and so ignited the main charge. All these events took time and the cumulative delay from the instant of pressing the trigger until actual ignition and explosion was small but, nevertheless, appreciable. With a moving target due allowance had to be made for this delay and this was not always an easy matter since the hangfire itself was not constant. Many gunmakers sought means to overcome this hangfire but without success.

Living in Scotland in the small parish of Belhelvie was a clergyman with an enquiring mind of a distinctly scientific nature and as he was also a keen shooter he sought means to reduce this hangfire which had cost him many a fine target. The Rev. Alexander Forsyth was an enterprising amateur chemist and he had, during his reading and correspondence, come across mention of chemicals which were so unstable that a sharp blow would cause them to explode. This group of chemicals, known as fulminates, included some that were readily available and Forsyth produced an ingenious gadget to utilise this explosive power. In place of the usual pan was a small, hollow, metal container known as the 'scent bottle' and into this was placed a quantity of fulminate. The internal design of the scent bottle was such that if inverted a few grains of fulminate found their way into the touchhole. Having deposited a few grains of fulminate the scent bottle was returned to its original position and this movement brought into position a spring loaded plunger so situated that the end was directly above the grains of fulminate. In place of a cock holding a piece of flint a solid metal hammer was fitted. As this swung forward it struck the spring loaded plunger and drove it downwards to strike the few grains of fulminate, the explosion of which produced a small flash sufficient to penetrate the touchhole and ignite the main charge.

The adoption of a system of ignition which depended upon chemical rather than mechanical means did not have an immediate impact on firearms design for Forsyth's mechanical system was complex, a little unreliable and even dangerous. However, once the principle had been established gunsmiths and chemists began to experiment with ideas for improving and simplifying the original system. One basic problem was that of ensuring that the explosive compound, mercuric fulminate was the most common, was available in compact, manageable quantities which could easily and safely be placed in the correct position to ignite the main charge of powder. Experiments were numerous and the fulminate was compounded with various fixatives such as gum, to produce small balls of detonating compound; other makers preferred to place the powder in small quills, small flat, copper caps or paper caps. However nearly all systems suffered from sundry disadvantages, not least being the difficulty of handling tiny capsules or pellets when in the field.

The system which gained widest acceptance was the percussion cap and this consisted of a small copper cylinder, closed at one end. On the inside of the closed end was deposited a small amount of the detonating compound. This small copper cylinder was placed over a projecting spigot known as the 'nipple' and held in place by friction. The nipple was drilled through with a small diameter hole which led directly to the main charge. The lock of the gun was fitted with a large, solid nosed hammer which, when released by the trigger, swung forward, struck the metal cap and detonated the percussion compound so that the flash passed, via the hole, to detonate the main charge.

The question of who first produced the copper percussion cap is one which has not been finally settled by firearms historians. Many famous gunmakers and shooters laid claim to this honour, Manton of London, Hawker the great shooter, the Frenchman Prelat, all had strong claims and recently discovered evidence suggests that Durs Egg, one of the most famous of London gunmakers, may have been one of the first. However, the honour is usually accredited to an Englishman, Joshua Shaw, who went to live in America, and claimed to have invented the cap about 1815 although he did not take out or claim a patent until 1822.

No matter to whom the honour of invention belongs, the adoption of the copper cap opened the way for a number of changes in the gun trade, both in design and production. Without doubt the percussion cap offered a number of very great advantages; it was small but not too small to be handled with a minimum of difficulty even in bad weather or under war conditions. Hangfire was reduced and the system was reliable with the rate of misfire certainly far less than with the old flint mechanism. Another great advantage of this system was that flintlock weapons could be converted to take the new system with a minimum of work. Generally speaking a 'drum and pillar' conversion was most often carried out, whereby the touchhole was reamed out and a small, drilled block of metal screwed firmly into its place and from this drum of metal projected the nipple and the barrel was then ready to use the cap. From the cock the frizzen and frizzen-spring were removed and also the old flint cock and in its place was put a solid nosed hammer. On many weapons the nipple was fitted directly into the barrel and an offset hammer used to strike the cap. Simplicity of construction gave the designer and gunmaker much greater freedom for there was no longer any need for bulky frizzens and springs and the solid hammer was far cheaper and simpler to make. Birmingham and Liège, in Belgium, began to produce quantities of cheap but, within their limits, quite satisfactory weapons. Percussion pocket pistols became very common whilst the greater freedom afforded to the designer was reflected by the vastly increased output of multibarrelled weapons. Pistols with two and four barrels were produced in bulk and became very common at this period.

The fairly obvious virtues of the percussion system were not necessarily immediately apparent to the military and although percussion caps were in use in the 1820s most European armies did not adopt the system until the 1830s. Caution on the part of the authorities was understandable for often considerations other than efficiency were involved. Obviously no Government wished to become involved in vast and unnecessary expense and what was wanted by most military authorities was a simple and efficient system which would allow them to convert their flintlock weapons to the new system. In 1831 the British Army really began producing its first percussion weapons although the flintlock, the 'Brown Bess' was still to see service in many parts of the world for years to come.

As already pointed out, simplicity of construction resulted in an increased output of cheaper weapons but it also permitted the development of mass production methods. As a result of various military shortcomings shown up during the Crimean War, the British Government decided to expand its own manufacturing centre and thus was born the famous Enfield Small Arms factory. Efficient machinery was introduced and rifled barrels which until the time of the Industrial Revolution had been laboriously produced by manual means, were now capable of fairly rapid mechanical production. Labour force and costs were greatly reduced and the government was largely released from its dependence on civilian contractors.

One weapon which probably owes its development more to the percussion cap than anything else was the revolver. This type of weapon was by no means new, examples are known which date back to the 16th century, but the wheel-lock and flintlock systems did not readily lend themselves to the production of simple, multi-shot weapons. However, the small percussion cap and nipple made design far simpler and it fell to a Yankee from Connecticut, Samuel Colt, to produce a really practical percussion revolver. He patented his design in England in December 1835 and in the U.S.A. in February 1836. His initial success was very small indeed and at one time it looked as if he might well go out of business but thanks to the proven value of his revolver; in numerous campaigns such as the Seminole Wars and with the help of a Texas Ranger friend of his, Captain Samuel Walker; Samuel Colt gained contracts large enough to justify the expenditure of money in setting up his own factory. From then on Colt and revolver became almost synonymous. In 1849 he produced his famous and very popular Pocket revolver, which fired a ·31 bullet and set the pattern for the next decade or so. In 1851 he produced the famous and possibly the most popular of his weapons, the so-called Navy Belt pistol or Old Model Navy. This was a six shot percussion revolver firing a ·36 bullet from a $7\frac{1}{2}$ inch barrel. The long barrel gave it a good degree of accuracy whilst the ·36 calibre bullet was suitable for most general purposes. The success of his pistols was outstanding and Samuel Colt, who could never be called modest, made sure that the world knew of its success. In 1851 the Great Exhibition was held in London at which examples of the manufacturer's art and ingenuity were displayed to an amazed and enthusiastic public. Samuel Colt took the opportunity to visit England and presented his pistols, which had been on exhibition at the great show, to any distinguished British personality whom he thought might be of the slightest use to him in promoting the sales of his product. So confident was Colt of his success that in 1851 he actually set up a London factory to manufacture as well as assemble parts supplied by his American factory. Colt found that his sales were below his expectations and by 1886/7 production had virtually ceased.

As may be imagined English gunmakers did not welcome the intrusion of a foreign competitor into their home market and many and bitter were the exchanges between Colt and manufacturers of revolvers in London and Birmingham.

By the 1860s a number of British gunsmiths were well known for the very fine quality of their percussion revolvers. These English revolvers were, generally speaking, of better decorative quality than Colt's products and varied from his weapons in many details. Generally they were more adventurous than Colt who stuck very much to his basic design, but English gunsmiths tended to experiment and produced a variety of models.

About the middle of the 19th century a simpler form of percussion revolver was being produced known as the 'pepper box'. This differed from a conventional revolver in that each of the five or six charges operated in its own barrel; a circular block of metal was drilled with five or six bores each of which was connected at the rear to a nipple and this whole cylinder block rotated about a central axis. Most of these pepperboxes, although by no means all, were fitted with a double action mechanism which means that pressure on the trigger caused the cylinder to rotate, raised a flat bar hammer and, if the pressure was continued, eventually disengaged the bar which fell to strike the cap. Pressure on the trigger was then released and repeated to rotate the cylinder again and bring the next unfired charge into position. These pepperboxes were fairly common although they often varied in minor details of design and construction. They were essentially self-defence weapons being fairly inaccurate at all but short ranges.

Efficient though the percussion revolver and pepperbox were they did suffer, as did all firearms of this period, from one great disadvantage for loading was rather slow and inconvenient. With both artillery and hand-guns a quantity of powder had to be poured down the barrel, or into the breech, followed by a wad, followed by the ball and perhaps another wad. This took time and in the changing circumstances of warfare rapidity of fire was beginning to play an important part. What was required was some simple method of loading the chamber or cylinder with a minimum of time wasted and a maximum convenience.

Cartridges, like revolvers, had been used from the very beginning of firearms history. Early examples mostly consisted of paper cylinders holding an appropriate charge of powder and a bullet; the paper was torn and the powder poured down the barrel to be followed by the paper acting as a wad and finally the ball. Efforts were made to manufacture a cartridge which could be loaded in at the breach and did not require tearing or altering in any way.

It was not until about 1838 when von Dreyse produced his cartridge with an enclosed primer which was struck and detonated by a needle operated by a bolt, that a practical system became possible. About the same time Lefaucheaux, a French maker, was experimenting with a 'pin-fire' mechanism. This consisted of a small metal rod, one end of which rested on a percussion cap set in the base of a paper cartridge. The rod projected through a small slot in the barrel and was struck by the hammer to explode the cap and ignite the charge. Originally this pin-fire cartridge was made of paper but later versions used metal cases. The other type of cartridge which proved popular was the 'rim-fire' where the fulminate was deposited on the inside end of the cartridge and was struck by the hammer of the gun. By the 1860s metal cased cartridges with a primer mounted at the centre of the base, were being produced and the modern cartridge firearm had arrived.

At the turn of the century the automatic, self-loading pistol came into being, when in 1893 the Borchardt pistol was produced. This weapon was eventually modified by George Luger and became one of the most famous of all automatic pistols. Strictly speaking such weapons should be called self-loading weapons for the true automatic will continue firing as long as the trigger is depressed. Machine guns also appeared about the same time as self-loading pistols and with these the firearm had reached its present-day form. Future developments are likely to be in degrees of efficiency, size of ammunition and rate of fire.

Guns

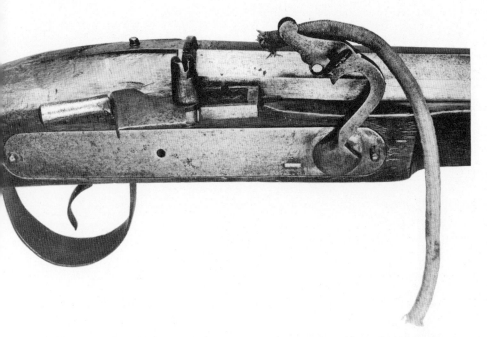

G.1.   A glowing match held in the jaws of the serpentine, swung forward to ignite the priming powder held in the pan, which fired the main charge of this English military musket. Early 17th century.

G.2.   The matchlock was used in the Orient much later than in Europe. This small Japanese matchlock has its iron barrel decorated with dragons, the lock is silvered and the wooden stock covered with black lacquer. 19th century.

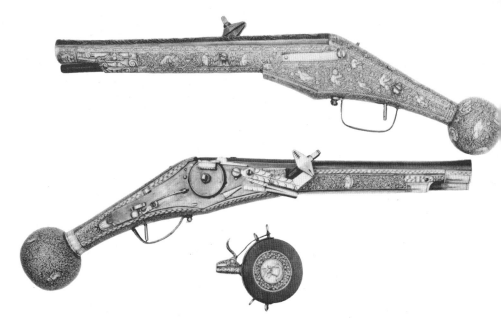

G.3.   TOP: This ball-butted wheel-lock pistol has a chiselled barrel and the stock is covered with engraved horn scroll work. Made in Thuringia (Germany). Late 16th century. Length 22 inches. CENTRE: Similar pistol, probably made by Klaus Hirt of Wasungen (Germany). The barrels and locks retain their original deep blue colouring on both weapons. Length 23 inches. BOTTOM: Flask for the fine priming powder, decorated with silver and horn strapwork. Diameter 3 inches. Last quarter of 16th century.

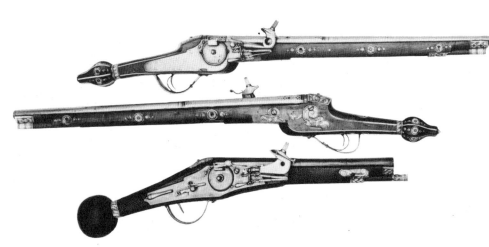

G.4.   TOP CENTRE: Pair of straight stocked wheel-lock pistols made by Hans Stockmann of Dresden in early 17th century. The stocks have inset panels of engraved horn. Length 30 inches. BOTTOM: Saxon wheel-lock pistol with straighter stock and much less decoration than those in G.3. The wood of the stock has been worked to look like horn. Length $22\frac{1}{2}$ inches. Last quarter of 16th century.

G.5. G.5A. Made around 1590 this wheel-lock pistol, only 13 inches long, was possibly made for a boy. It is decorated with the walnut stock inlaid and much of the metal work gilded.

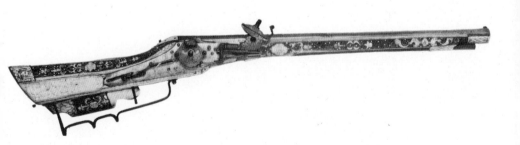

G.6. The wheel-lock mechanism is here fitted to a carbine, overall length 32 inches. The butt has a curved cheek piece because the weapon was placed by the side of the face when firing. This weapon has a rifled barrel (8 grooves) and would probably be quite accurate. S. German. c. 1590.

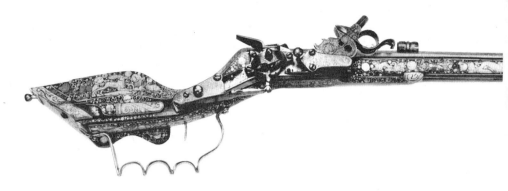

G.7.   A distinctive style of wheel-lock, known as a Tschinke, was produced in Silesia. This example, dating from the middle 17th century, has most of the features including inlaid decoration and the peculiar construction of the mechanism with exposed main spring. The rifled barrel (6 grooves) has a tubular backsight.

G.8.   These pistols, dating from the late 18th century, are fitted with the snaphaunce lock which first appeared in the 16th century. This ignition system was used by many Italian gunmakers long after the rest of Europe had abandoned it. Note the fine quality metalwork, a feature of many Italian firearms. Overall length 13½ inches. Locks dated 1792.

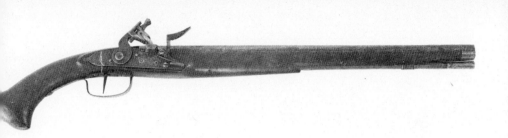

G.9. Most 17th century holster flintlock pistols have very long barrels as here. The flat cock and lock plate, the oval section butt and small steel pommel cap are common in pistols of the mid-17th century. Lock engraved ROB. SILK and fitted with the hook-like catch (dog), often found on English flintlocks of this period.

G.10. A dog lock is also fitted to this English musket made 1640–50. These weapons were long (63 inches overall) and so heavy that a support (the rest) was needed to keep it steady when firing.

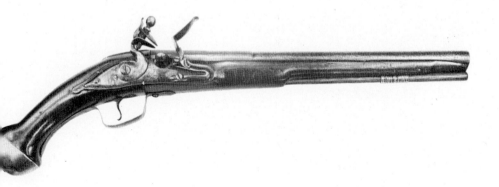

G.11. This military flintlock pistol has brass fittings and a characteristic hemispherical butt cap. On the lock plate is engraved the cypher J II R of James II of England. Overall length 21 inches. c. 1685.

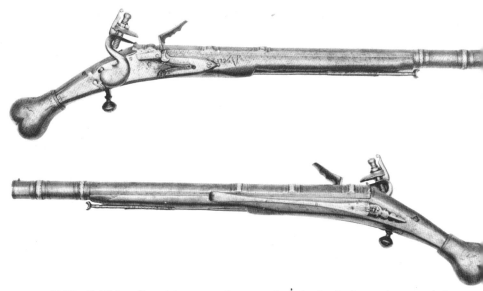

G.12. G.12A. Scottish gunmakers produced pistols in a characteristic style; dating from the late 17th century, this has the usual all-metal stock and the side hook from which the pistol was hung from the belt. The heart-shaped butt is a feature of early Scottish pistols but the button trigger is found on pistols of the 18th and 19th century.

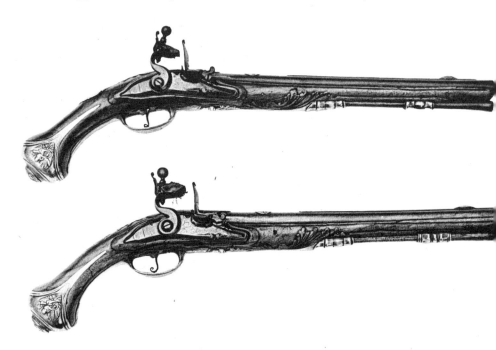

G.13. Pair of holster pistols of early 18th century with brass furniture including butt cap with long side spurs, common features of this period. Like the blunderbuss in Plate G.14 the lock plate has a 'banana' shape and the stock has some simple carving—again common features of around 1700. Flemish. Overall length 21 inches. Bore ·6 inches.

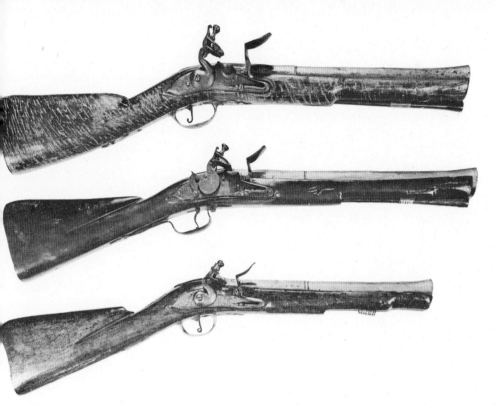

G.14. TOP: A brass-barrelled blunderbuss by DOLEP dating from about 1690 with 'banana' shaped lock plate. Overall length 30¼ inches, barrel 16 inches. Diameter at muzzle 1½ inches. MIDDLE: This blunderbuss, dating from about 1680, was made by ROB-SILKE (See plate G.9) who was Master of the London Gunmakers Company from 1696–7. The dog-lock and flat lock plate are characteristic of this period. Overall length 30¼ inches, barrel 16 inches. Diameter at muzzle 1½ inches. BOTTOM: Another blunderbuss with brass barrel made by W. NUTT about 1685. Like the others it has the rather chunky look of so many blunderbusses of this period. Overall length 27½ inches, barrel 13½ inches. Diameter at muzzle 1⅜ inches.

G.15. Wheel-lock pistols were carried by cavalrymen until the late 17th century and most were plain like this example. This pistol is rifled (8 grooves) and has some simple inlaid decoration on the butt. Overall length 28 inches. German 17th century.

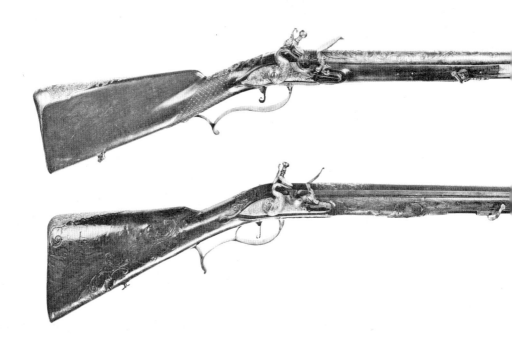

G.16.   TOP: Flintlock fowling piece originating in Carlsbad in Bohemia
with chiselled decoration on the barrel and lock plate. The lock plate is
'banana' shaped but is slightly rounded unlike the earlier examples which
were flatter. Barrel length 51½ inches. Bohemia c. 1700. BOTTOM: This
sporting rifle (4 grooves) dates from about 1750 and the change in the
shape of the lockplate is obvious. The walnut stock has some carved
decoration and the steel fittings are embellished with low relief chiselling.
Barrel length 41½ inches. German.

G.17. A pair of French pocket pistols made by MAHAY of Paris, c. 1740.
The stepped barrels are decorated with gold damascening and the breech
and walnut butts are inlaid with silver wire. Overall length 6½ inches.

G.18. This lock on an early 18th century Italian fowling piece shows the quality of workmanship on such weapons. Chiselled steelwork was popular as a means of decoration. Triggers of this period commonly have a backward curl at their tip as here.

G.19. Most military weapons were fairly plain and rugged in construction. This French musket was made in Charleville, c. 1770, and has the usual muzzle and barrel bands which held the barrel firmly in place on the stock. The lock is plain and rings are fitted for the attachment of a sling.

G.20. Turkish and Balkan pistols differ from most European models in both shape and decoration. Many have a straight, long, thin appearance (known as rat-tail). The stock is of silver embossed with scrolls and other decoration. The lock is probably of German origin, bearing the inscription BERNS DORFER A ANSPACH. Overall length 23½ inches, barrel length 13 inches. Bore ·66 inches. Late 18th century.

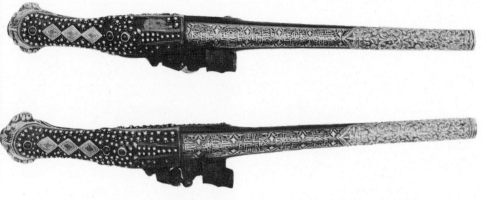

G.21. Decoration on Balkan pistols is often elaborate. This pair have inlaid gold inscriptions on the barrel, scroll work on the butts, embossed silver sheathing and semi-precious stones set in the butts.

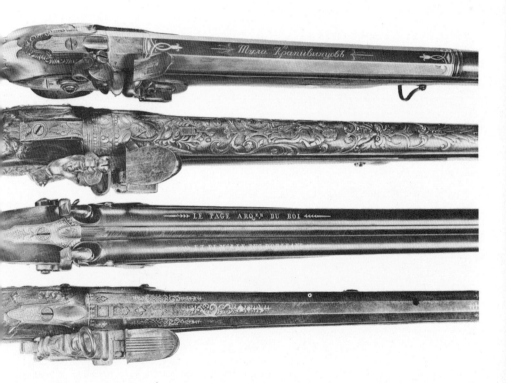

G.22. DECORATED BARRELS 1, Russian 12 bore flintlock c. 1820 made in Tula, has inlaid gold inscription on top rib. 2, made in Carlsbad this weapon has an elaborately chiselled barrel. 3, a double barrelled sporting gun has the barrels browned and the maker's name *Le Page* inlaid in gold. 4, a Spanish barrel has inlaid decoration and carries at the breech the stamped gold poinçon (inset mark) of FERNANDO OLAVE [of] PLACENTIA.

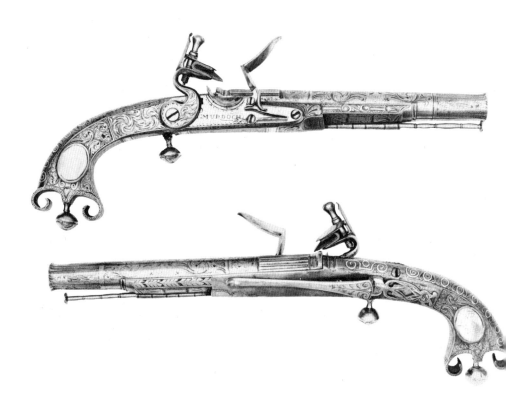

G.23.   All-steel Scottish pistols by I. MURDOCK of DOUNE—a town renowned for its gunmakers. The stocks are embellished with scrollwork, the ball trigger is silver and the oval escutcheon on the butts is engraved with the name G. DOWNE and the date 1781. Overall length 12½ inches.

G.24. TOP: Most flintlock weapons were single shot and many efforts
were made to overcome this; probably the most common system was that
using two barrels. Selection of barrels was made by the 'tap' set in the
breech block. This pistol c. 1780 bears the name of the maker T. BARKER
and WARRINGTON. BOTTOM: Intended mainly for self-protection many
small flintlock pistols (or pocket pistols) were made during the late 18th
century—this one is by BOND of London.

G.25.　Another popular device was the spring bayonet attached to the barrel of a pistol or blunderbuss. This pistol has a brass barrel widening at the muzzle and the bayonet, released by pulling back the trigger guard, swings forward to lock into place. The ramrod is fitted at the side of the barrel instead of underneath as is more usual. Made by PARKER of London c. 1800.

G.26.　Boxlock, flintlock pistol made by STANTON of London, c. 1780; the slabsided butt is decorated with inlaid silver wire. No ramrod was required as the barrel unscrewed to permit the powder and ball to be put directly into the breech. Barrel length 2·4 inches. Bore ·437 inches.

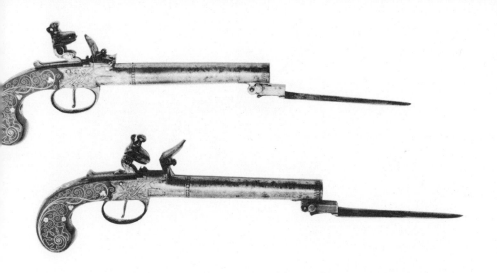

G.27. These pistols by WHEELER c. 1800, are fairly typical except the barrels are larger than normal on such weapons. Overall length 17 inches.

G.28. Detail of a pistol fitted with a spring bayonet showing how the point engaged with the sliding trigger guard and was released by pressing the rear trigger.

G.29. Detail of the breech of a brass barrel in a blunderbuss by BUNNEY. The place of origin, LONDON, is in script. The two marks at the side are the crossed sceptres and surmounting crown which show that the weapon had been proved by the British Board of Ordnance in the Tower of London.

G.29A. Lock of the blunderbuss showing the maker's name and the sliding bolt safety catch which held the action at a safe half-cock position.

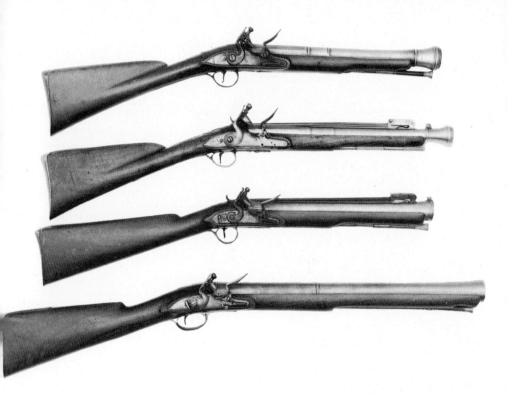

G.30.   Late 18th century blunderbusses used by mail coach guards and
for home defence. 1, brass barrel, walnut stock by GRICE, length 29¼
inches. 2, brass barrel and spring bayonet by KING, length 30½ inches.
3, brass barrel and spring bayonet by RICHARDS, length 29¾ inches.
4, brass barrel and fitted with simple dog catch on the lock, by JONES,
CORNHILL LONDON. Length 35¾ inches.

G.31.   Liège in Belgium was one of the great centres of arms manufacture
during the 19th century. This flintlock pistol is typical of early 19th
century Liège weapons with its square cut butt fitted with brass cap and
lanyard ring.

G.32 G.32A. Front and back views of a French cavalry pistol; the construction is simple and sturdy with a wooden butt and barrel and breech fashioned in one. Most French military weapons are designated by the year of adoption and this type is known as System 1777.

G.33. India Pattern Brown Bess with 39 inch barrel; the lock is engraved with the word TOWER and the crowned G.R. Brown Bess muskets were used for roughly a century from 1720 and saw service through much of the Napoleonic war period. The models varied in details—especially in length of barrel.

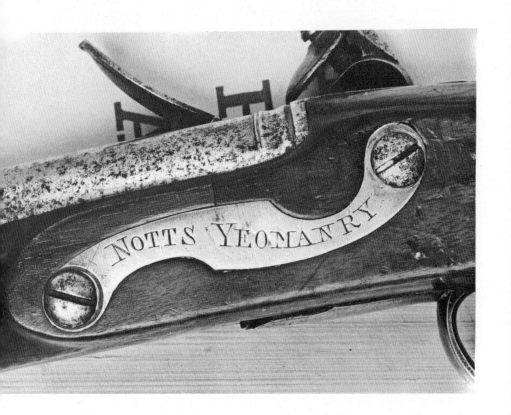

G.34. Many military weapons are identified by regimental or armoury
markings as on this flintlock pistol which has the side plate engraved. It
formed part of the equipment of a troop of the Nottinghamshire
Yeomanry; a part time cavalry force like many during the 18th and 19th
centuries.

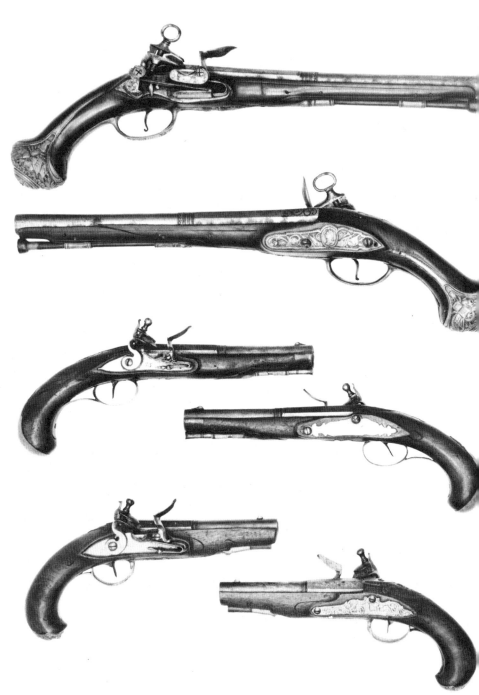

G.35. TOP: Pair of Spanish pistols $17\frac{1}{2}$ inches long, the barrels bear the mark of E UDAL P O US while the locks are marked DE OP. The ring on the top jaw is very common on Spanish flintlocks. Late 18th century. CENTRE: Austrian travelling pistol c. 1760 with blued barrel $9\frac{1}{2}$ inches long. BOTTOM: Pair of Austrian or German pistols 11 inches. They seem quite ordinary but the barrels are rifled. Late 18th century.

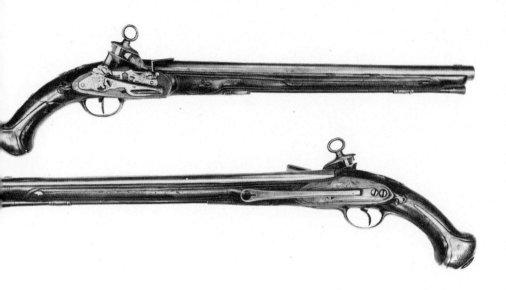

G.36.   Pair of long-barrelled Spanish pistols of late 18th century. Spanish locks, known as Miquelet, differ in their construction by having the main spring mounted on the outside of the lock plate. Their method of engaging full and half cock also differs from that of other European gunmakers.

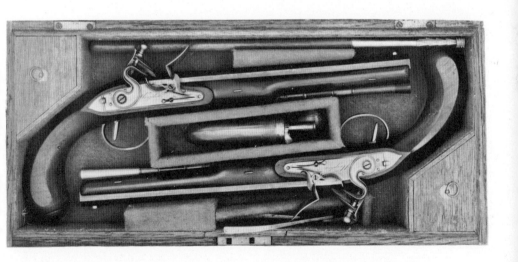

G.37.   In the late 18th century the specialised duelling pistol evolved, designed to provide a quick and accurate shot. In the interests of fairness they were usually supplied in pairs in a case. Made by WOGDEN, a London maker renowned for his duelling pistols, the case included powder flask, bullet mould and cleaning rods.

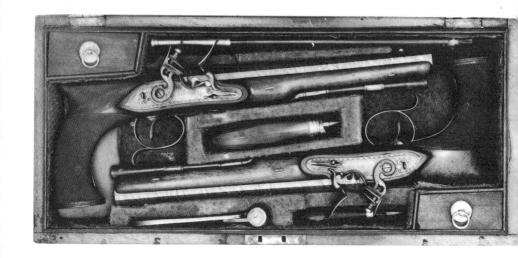

G.38.   Pair of duelling pistols by H. W. MORTIMER of early 19th century.
Unlike the pistols in G.37, these have saw-handled butts and spurs on the
trigger guard; both features intended to give a firmer, steadier grip. The
mahogany case contains all the usual accessories.

G.39.   Duelling pistols were normally very plain. At the other extreme
were these pistols designed for the Turkish and Balkan markets. Many
were locally made but others were produced in Europe for export.
TOP: Damascus barrel, stock inlaid with scrolling on coral and silver
mounts. 22 inches long. BOTTOM: One of a pair of Turkish pistols—fitted
with European barrels signed along top rib P DE SELIER MASTRIGHT
Silver gilt furniture.

G.40.   Many efforts were made to improve the efficiency or rate of fire of the flintlock. Henry Nock, a very famous London gunmaker, devised this lock which was completely enclosed and used no screws, being held together by clips and springs. This screwless lock is fitted to a Volunteer's pistol c. 1800 with a 9 inch brass barrel.

G.41   During the later 17th century a new magazine system was evolved, probably by a gunmaker in Bologna, but it is usually known as the Lorenzoni system after another gunmaker. Essentially it consisted of reservoirs of powder and balls in the butt, which were transferred to the breech by rotating a breech block operated by a handle set at the side of the breech. Pistol signed BARBAR LONDON. C. 1760.

G.42. Here the Lorenzoni type action has been re-stocked in the late 18th or early 19th century in a sporting gun, the octagonal barrel engraved MAGHIRA.

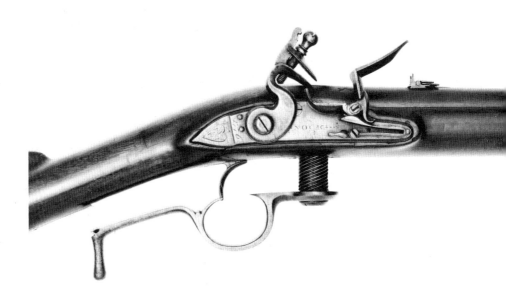

G.43. One of the most efficient breech loading systems was invented by Capt. Patrick Ferguson who gave a most convincing exhibition of its virtues in 1776. Powder and ball were loaded directly into the breech by way of a hole, exposed by rotating the trigger guard to unscrew a plug so allowing access. This Ferguson cavalry carbine was made by H. Nock for the East India Company. Overall length $44\frac{1}{2}$ inches.

G.44 G.44A. In 1818 Elisha Collier, an American, patented a system for a flintlock revolver. Originally the 5 shot cylinder was rotated automatically but Collier modified his design to make it hand turned. Overall length 47 inches.

G.45.　This pair of Irish pocket pistols, c. 1800, and made by TOMLINSON of DUBLIN, are fitted with a self priming device which consists of a magazine of powder fitted to the rear of the frizzen. The bar at the side is engraved INVENTED BY T. PATTISON DUBLIN. Overall length 9 inches, barrel $4\frac{7}{8}$ inches. Bore ·67 inches.

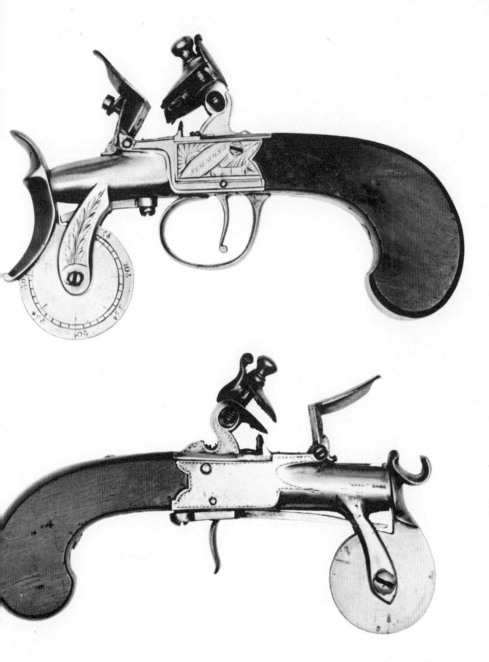

G.46. Gunpowder was an uncertain mixture and it was as well to test each batch if consistent performance of a gun was required. Simplest and most common were powder testers like these, where a small charge of powder was exploded to rotate a graduated wheel; the degree of rotation giving a comparative reading of the explosive strength.

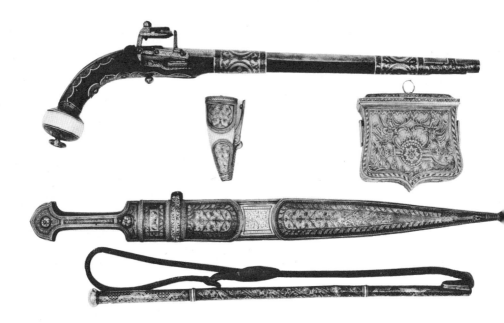

G.47. Cossack pistol with $14\frac{1}{2}$ inch barrel and a ball butt fashioned from walrus ivory; the stock is leather covered and the pistol has the usual ball trigger. BELOW an ivory powder measure with silver and gilt fittings decorated with niello; the cartridge box is similarly decorated. The broad bladed dagger, kindjhal, is a traditional Cossack weapon like the whip, both are decorated with silver and niello work.

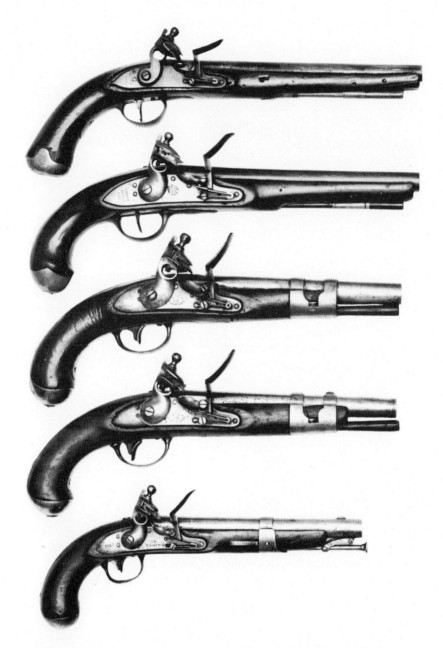

G.47/A. TOP TO BOTTOM 1, 1808 U.S. Army flintlock Martial pistol
with lock signed J HENRY PHILA. Overall length 16 inches. 2, 1808 U.S.
Navy flintlock pistol with lock bearing American eagle and U. States
and signed S NORTH BERLIN CON. Overall length 16½ inches. 3, 1816
U.S. Martial Pistol 9 inch barrel, overall length 15¼ inches. 4, 1816 U.S.
Martial pistol. Overall length 15½ inches. 5, 1827 U.S. Martial pistol,
lock stamped US S NORTH 1827. Overall length 13½ inches.

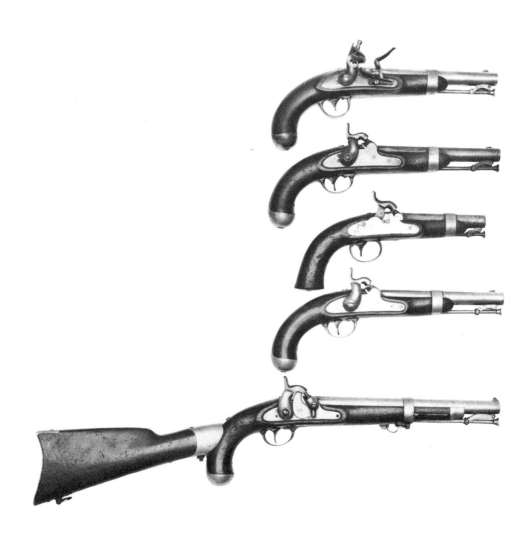

G.47/B. TOP TO BOTTOM 1, 1836 U.S. flintlock pistol with 8¼ inch barrel, lock inscribed US R JOHNSON MIDDN CONN 1842. Overall length 13¾ inches. 2, 1842 U.S. Percussion Army pistol. 8½ inch barrel. Lock stamped U S H ASTON MIDDTN CONN 1849. Overall length 14 inches. 3, 1842 U.S. Percussion Navy pistol, 6 inch barrel. Lock signed N.P. AMES SPRINGFIELD MASS. Overall length 11¼ inches. 4, 1842 U.S. Percussion Martial pistol dated 1853. Lock signed PALMETTA ARMORY SC and COLUMBIA SC 1852. Overall length 14 inches. 5, 1855 tape lock pistol carbine, 12 inch barrel with stock, the overall length is 28½ inches. American.

G.48. Fowling piece fitted with the Forsyth 'scent bottle' percussion device; on the top rib is FORSYTH & CO PATENT GUN MAKERS LONDON and it is half stocked in walnut. Overall length 46½ inches. c. 1816.

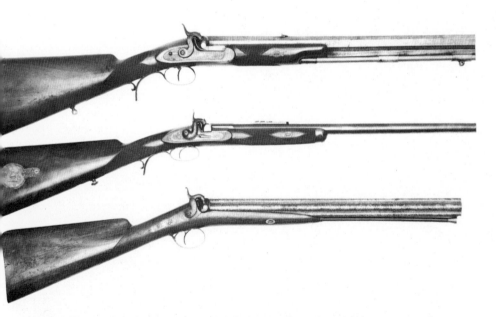

G.49. Percussion longarms. TOP: 4 bore sporting gun with brass ramrod and octagonal barrel. MIDDLE: Target rifle (six grooves) marked at breech, WHITWORTH PATENT NO. 271, c. 1860. BOTTOM: 7 barrelled rifle marked FORSYTH & CO PATENT GUN MAKER LONDON. These weapons, which discharged a volley of seven shots, were popular among wild fowlers.

G.50. By the mid-19th century the gun trade had evolved efficient
means for rifling barrels and they became more common. TOP: Canadian
target rifle by W. P. MARSTON of TORONTO, half stocked with steel
furniture and fitted with a full length telescopic sight made by MORGAN
JAMES of UTICA N.Y. Barrel 33 inches. c. 1860. BOTTOM: Pennsylvanian
long rifle (c.f.Pl.G.51) with heavy octagonal barrel, 7 groove rifling,
marked CHARLESTON SO C.A. (South Carolina). c. 1850. Barrel 36¾
inches.

G.51. Pennsylvanian or Kentucky rifles. TOP TO BOTTOM. 1, double
barrelled flintlock with nickel-silver furniture, walnut stock. Overall
length 48½ inches. Late 18th century. 2, 7 groove rifling with lock marked
BARNETT. Overall length 56¼ inches. Late 18th century. 3, octagonal
barrel marked T.BENNETT, stained walnut stock. Overall length 63½
inches. Late 18th or early 19th century. 4, flintlock converted to percussion,
the barrel signed H. CARLISLE and lock signed ASHMORE. Overall
length 57½ inches. 5, percussion, barrel marked LEMAN LANCASTER PA
(Pennsylvania). Overall length 55 inches. 6, percussion, stock decorated
with inlaid silver fish. Overall length 55¾ inches. 7, percussion with barrel
marked D. ROTHROCK and lock signed JOSEPH GOLCHER. Overall
length 55½ inches. c. 1830.

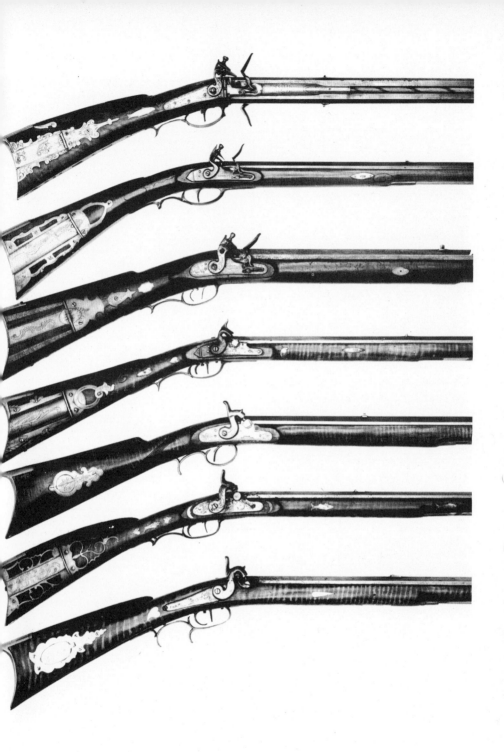

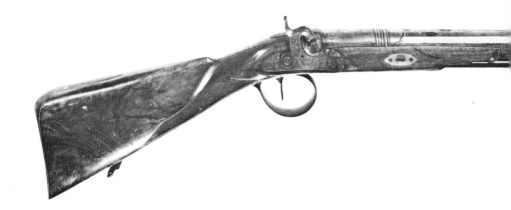

G.52. German 10 bore gun fitted with a Persian twist, 16 sided barrel. The half stock of walnut is fitted with a cheek piece and the furniture is all of steel, with the unusual feature that the side plate repeats the lock plate in shape and decoration. Barrel length $42\frac{1}{2}$ inches. c. 1840.

G.53. German 19 bore, half stocked sporting gun with a back action lock; the gold escutcheon plate bears the crowned monogram of a Count of the Holy Roman Empire. All furniture including the lock, is chiselled in low relief. Barrel length $40\frac{1}{2}$ inches. Second quarter of 19th century.

G.54. The percussion cap enabled gunmakers to produce a tremendous
variety of multi-shot weapons, such as this side by side, double-barrelled
pistol by WESTLEY RICHARDS, 170 NEW BOND ST, LONDON. The barrel
assembly was partially rotated to bring each nipple into line with the bar
hammer.

G.55. Grouping a number of chambers in a block produced the pepperbox and this is an example of the most common form. Action was automatic and pressure on the trigger rotated the cylinder block, raised the bar
hammer and allowed it to fall and fire each of the six shots in turn.
Overall length 8 inches. Barrel 3 inches.

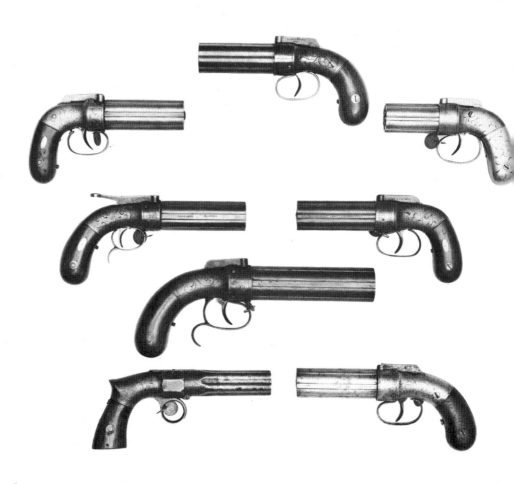

G.56. Selection of American pepperboxes, all mid-19th century. TOP
CENTRE: 6 shot by Allen & Thurber No. 3269. TOP LEFT: 6 shot by
Allen & Thurber. TOP RIGHT: 6 shot by Allen & Thurber with nickel
silver grips. 2ND ROW LEFT: 6 shot by Stocking & Co., Patented 1848.
2ND ROW RIGHT: 6 shot. Allens patent. 3RD ROW CENTRE: 6 shot by
Allen & Thurber 1837. $10\frac{1}{4}$ inches long. BOTTOM ROW LEFT: 5 shot by
Robbins and Laurence. BOTTOM ROW RIGHT: 6 shot by Allen &
Thurber $7\frac{1}{2}$ inches long.

G.57.   TOP: 5 shot percussion revolver with side rammer. Weapons like these were mass produced by factories in Birmingham and Liège. BOTTOM: 5 shot, double trigger revolver by William Tranter and retailed by H. BECKWITH of LONDON. The part of the trigger below the trigger guard, cocks the action and rotates the cylinder while the firing mechanism is activated by the top section. Patented 1853.

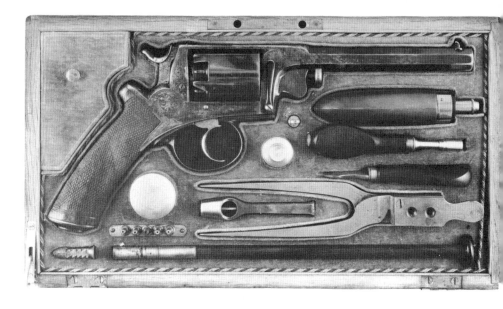

G.58. One of the most popular of British percussion revolvers was the Beaumont Adams but this example is a German copy. The velvet lined case differs from the British as the compartments are shaped to fit the accessories. Mid-19th century and marked on top strap IMPERIAL PATENT REVOLVER.

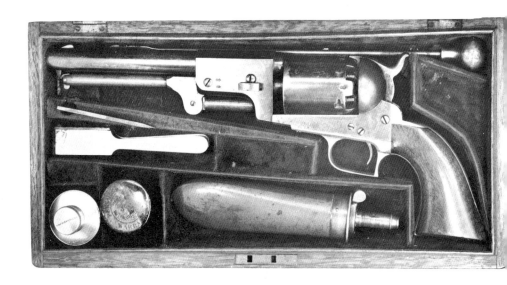

G.59. 2nd Model Dragoon revolver. They had a $7\frac{1}{2}$ inch barrel and fired a ·44 bullet, while the cylinder was engraved with a battle between Indians and soldiers. This bears London proof marks and is complete in its case lined in crimson velvet. Overall length 14 inches. Weight 4 lbs 2 ozs. It is marked on the barrel ADDRESS SAM. COLT NEW YORK CITY 9109.

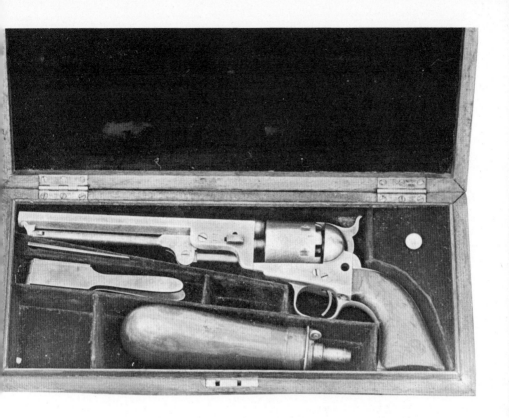

G.60.   One of the most popular of Colt's revolvers was the 'Navy'. Its long barrel, 7½ inches made for accuracy and its calibre ·36 inches was satisfactory for most purposes. The six shot cylinder was engraved with a naval combat scene. This specimen bears an Enfield stamp on the grip suggesting that it might have been part of an official British order.

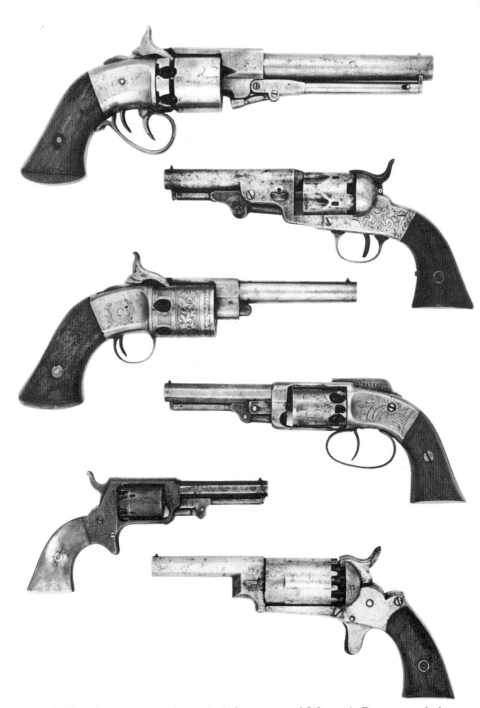

G.61.   American revolvers. 1, 6 shot stamped Warner's Patent, made by Springfield Arms Co.—front trigger rotates cylinder, rear one fires the shot. 2, 5 shot by B. J. HART & BRO. N.Y. 3, another by Springfield Arms Co. 6 chambers and stamped JAQUITHS PATENT 1838. 4, 5 shot stamped ELLIS PATENT. 5, 6 shot by BLISS AND GOODYEAR NEW HAVE CT. c. 1859. 6, 10 shot superimposed load revolver WALCH-FIREARMS CO NEW YORK.

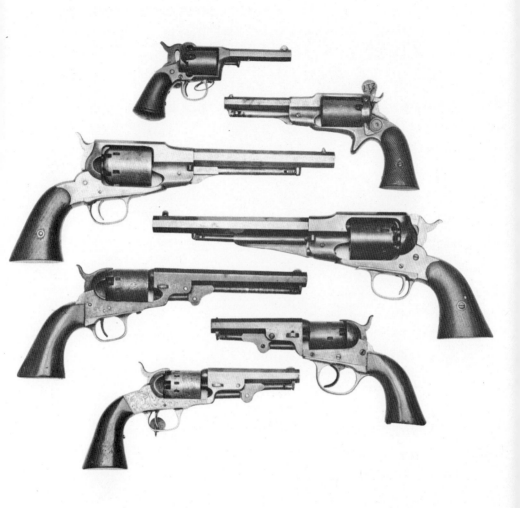

G.62. American made revolvers. 1, Beals' 1st Model, 5 shot, ·31, (patented in 1857) single piece rubber grip. 2, Beals' 3rd Model ·31 calibre. 3, Beals' Navy revolver ·36 patented 1859. 4, Remington New Model Army. 14½ inches overall. 5, Manhattan Arm Co. Navy revolver. 11½ inches overall. c. 1860. 6, Double action Cooper's percussion revolver c. 1865—very similar in appearance to a Colt. 7, a very rare pocket revolver made by THE LONDON PISTOL COMPANY which was a trade name of the Manhattan Firearms Co. Only 1000 were made.

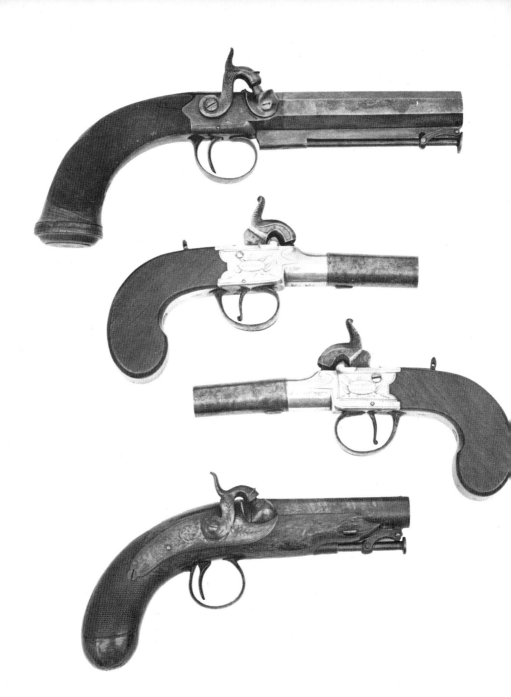

G.63. 1, conventional single shot percussion pistol by DUDLEY
PORTSMOUTH. c. 1840. 2, 3, many flintlocks were converted to take the
new percussion cap as with this pair of boxlock pistols. 8 inches overall by
SOMERS AND STANLEY LONDON. c. 1840. 4, percussion pistol by
TRULOCK & SON DUBLIN fitted with a back action lock and swivel
ramrod. c. 1840.

G.64. Small percussion pocket pistol by RIGBY of DUBLIN. The back strap of the butt is hinged and when raised reveals a space designed to hold ball and caps. Overall length 6 inches, barrel 2 inches.

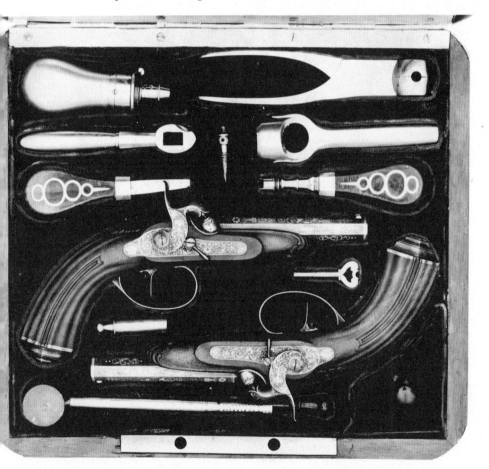

G.65. Pair of small travelling pistols, cased with all accessories, powder flask, wad cutters, rods and tools. The octagonal barrels are browned and inlaid with gold and silver, the locks are fitted with a patent safety device. Barrels signed I. ADAM KURCHENREUTER IN REGENSBURG c. 1830.

G.66.   Pair of flintlock duelling pistols by DURS EGG made about 1800 but later converted to the percussion system. Since the case is fitted out in the contoured, continental style, perhaps the conversion was carried out in France. The powder flask is also French in style.

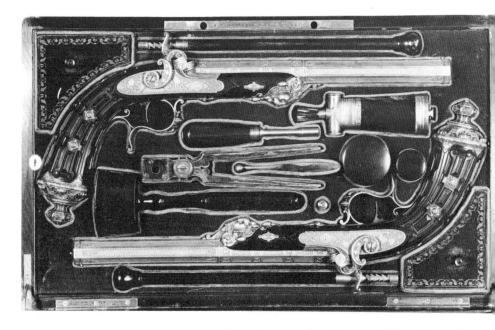

G.67.   Pair of target or duelling pistols with polygrove rifling, the stocks of ebony and the metalwork chiselled and embellished with gold. The case is bound in brass and lined with red velvet. Locks are inscribed GAUVAIN BART DU MONTMARNASSE 47.

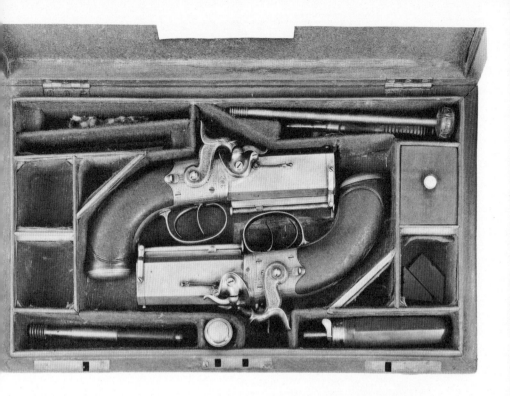

G.68.   Unusual pair of over and under, double barrelled rifled pistols by
THOMAS POTTS 70 MINORIES LONDON; the barrels are fashioned from
one slab-sided block of bronze. The pistol has nipple guards which were
designed to hold in position a type of cap known as top hat caps. Case is
lined with green baize. c. 1830.

G.69.   Prussian cavalry pistol of 1850, the lock marked POTSDAM below
a crown; the butt is fitted with a lanyard ring. The foresight blade is very
pronounced, a poor design feature. Overall length 15 inches, bore 15·6
inches.

G.70. All steel 12 mm, 6 shot, double action pin-fire revolver decorated overall with gold damascening in designs of leaves and vines. As there is no guard the trigger is folded up when not required, to reduce chances of accidental discharge. Overall length $10\frac{1}{4}$ inches. Barrel $5\frac{1}{4}$ inches.

G.71. Designed as a repeating weapon, the Treeby chain gun was patented in 1855 and 1858. The chambers each held one charge and were joined in a continuous belt. The barrel moves back and locks in place to make a good seal with the cylinder. Barrel 29 inches.

G.72. Combined sword/pistols were popular weapons. This Elgin cutlass pistol was patented in 1837. The barrel is octagonal and marked ELGIN'S PATENT. Overall length 17⅜ inches.

G.73. Pocket-knife pistols were also popular, if somewhat impractical. This example is designed to take a small pin-fire cartridge. The bar hammer on the right is operated by the trigger (bottom centre). Length of barrel 1·4 inches. Length of knife 3·5 inches.

G.74. The appearance of metal cartridges around the mid-19th century stimulated gunmakers to produce many new types of firearms. This 10 shot, 6 mm self defence pistol with its original leather purse holster, was known as a Squeezer and was held in the clenched fist with the barrel projecting between the middle fingers. Overall length 4½ inches. French, dated 1878.

G.75. Somewhat similar in action to G.74 is this Gaulois squeezer pistol. It held six 8 mm cartridges and could be concealed in the leather cigar case. Overall length 5⅛ inches. French. c. 1880.

G.76. One of the smallest automatic or self loading pistols ever produced is this KOLIBRI pistol using a 2·7 mm cartridge. Overall length 2⅞ inches. Barrel 1½ inches. c. 1914.

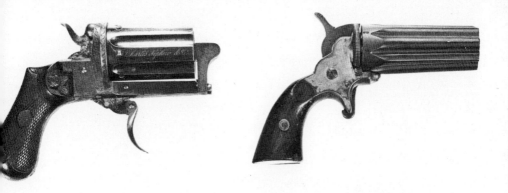

G.77. Metal cartridges considerably simplified the production of revolvers of many types. LEFT: ·32 centre fire, 6 shot 'pepperbox' revolver engraved CHARLES NEPHEW & CO CALCUTTA, folding trigger. Overall length 5½ inches. Barrel 2 inches. RIGHT: ·22 rim-fire, 8 shot, single-action American revolver. Overall length 5¼ inches. Barrel 2¾ inches. Late 19th century.

G.77/A. TOP RIGHT: ·22 pocket pistol with silvered barrel by T. J. STAFFORD NEW HAVEN CT. 1860. TOP LEFT: ·30 teat fire pocket revolver, CONN. ARMS CO NORFOLK CONN on barrel, 6 shot. c. 1867. CENTRE RIGHT: ·32 rim-fire revolver, on barrel B. A. CO. 5 shot. BOTTOM LEFT: ·41 colt, clover leaf 4 shot revolver (so named from the shape of the cylinder). 1871. BOTTOM RIGHT: My Friend knuckleduster pistol. 1866.

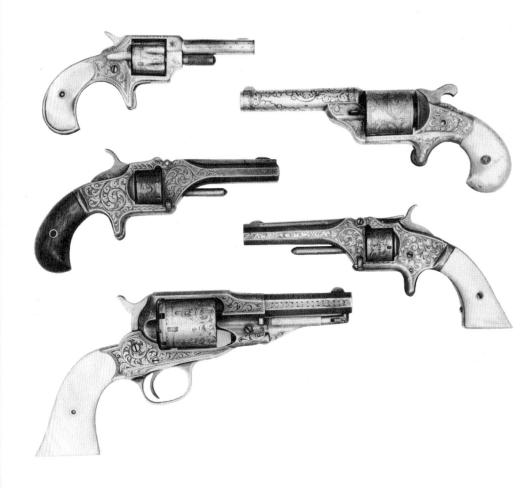

G.77/B. TOP LEFT: ·22 Remington pocket revolver, stamped on barrel
E. REMINGTON & SON ILION N.Y., 7 shot, gilded overall. Overall length
5¾ inches. c. 1880. TOP RIGHT: ·30 Moore's patent revolver. 6 shot gold
plated, mother of pearl grip. Overall length 7¼ inches. c. 1864. CENTRE
LEFT: ·22 pocket revolver, stamped on barrel AETNA ARMS CO NEW
YORK, 7 shot, brass frame. 1885. CENTRE RIGHT: ·22 pocket revolver
stamped SMITH & WESSON SPRINGFIELD MASS. 7 shot. c. 1864.
BOTTOM LEFT: ·36 rim-fire Remington New Model. Police revolver
converted from percussion to cartridge. 5 shot.

G.78.   TOP LEFT: 11·33 mm. Wall revolver with 20 shot cylinder No. 1
the grip very short and the trigger fitted with a lanyard ring. Belgium
c. 1870. TOP RIGHT: 30 shot pin-fire revolver with over and under barrels.
Belgium c. 1860. BOTTOM LEFT: 7 mm. Apache pistol stamped LDOLNE
INVAR; built in the form of a knuckleduster, pivoted blade. c. 1870.
BOTTOM RIGHT: 10 shot turret pistol by Noel, stamped J. F. COUREY
CANAT & CIE PARIS and SYSTEME A NOEL BTE S.G.D.G. c. 1860.

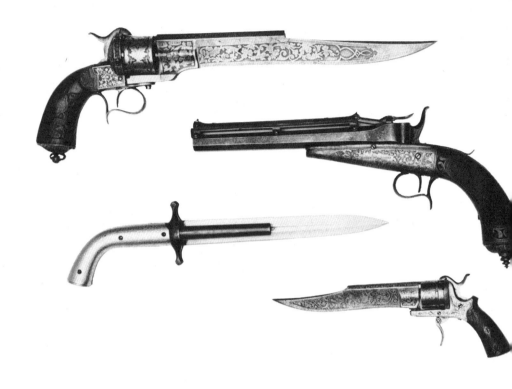

G.79. TOP LEFT: 11·5 mm knife pistol, blade etched, signed at breech DU MONTHIER. 6 shot, c. 1865. CENTRE RIGHT: Gravity fed revolver, with semi-tubular magazine above the barrel, ebony butt. c. 1870. BOTTOM LEFT: Double-barrelled percussion pistol sword, blade signed DU MONTHLIER BREVET/DUN—the barrels mounted either side of the blade. Barrels $3\frac{1}{4}$ inches. Overall length $14\frac{1}{4}$ inches. c. 1850. BOTTOM RIGHT: Pin-fire knife revolver, stamped DU MONTHIER B.S.G. D.G.510 6 shot, c. 1860. All these weapons are of French make.

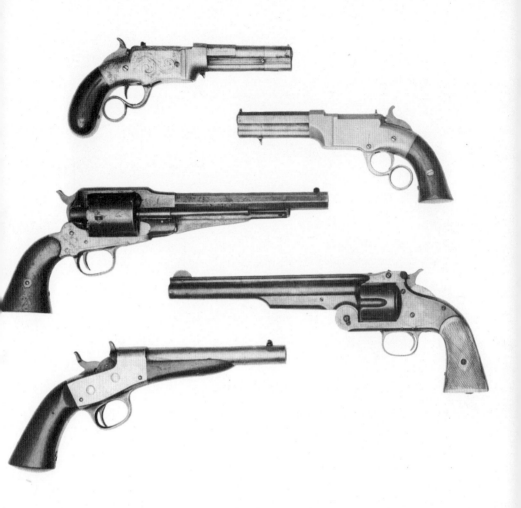

G.80. ·30 Volcanic pistol signed on barrel SMITH & WESSON NORWICH CT. C. 1854. This was a forerunner of the famous Winchester rifle. TOP RIGHT: Another ·30 volcanic pistol with more common octagonal barrel. Both have underbarrel magazines. Stamped NEW HAVEN CONN. PATENT FEB 14 1854. CENTRE LEFT: ·46 Remington New Model Army Revolver—converted from percussion to pin-fire. c. 1869. BOTTOM RIGHT: ·44 Army revolver by Smith and Wesson. 6 shot with ivory grip. 1871. BOTTOM LEFT: Remington ·5, 1867 Navy pistol. 7 inch barrel.

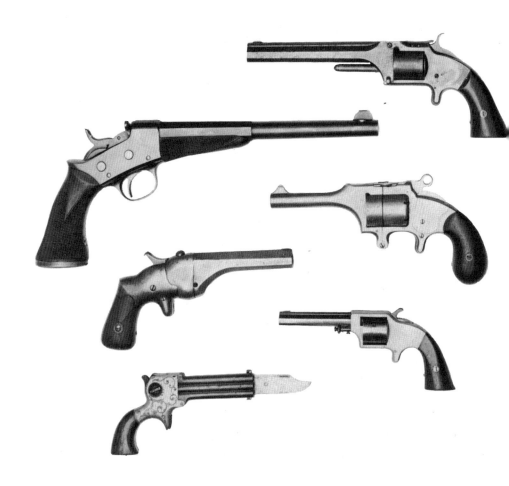

G.81. TOP RIGHT: ·32 old model no. 2 Army revolver, by Smith &
Wesson. 1868. TOP LEFT: ·22 target pistol with barrel stamped
REMINGTON ARMS CO. ILION N.Y. U.S.A. 1866, but nitro proved 1901–9.
CENTRE RIGHT: Crispin's ·32 centre fire revolver. 6 shot. patented in
1868 in Britain and 1863 in U.S.A. CENTRE LEFT: ·44 'Bull dog' pistol
signed on barrel CONNECTICUT ARMS AND MANF'G CO. NANBUG CONN
patented 1864. BOTTOM RIGHT: ·30 cartridge revolver inscribed EAGLE
ARMS CO NEW YORK. 6 shot 1868. BOTTOM LEFT: ·22 rim-fire knife
pistol with 3 barrels—blade slides out, made by NEWHAVEN ARMS CO.
1861.

Edged Weapons

Although a few gaps and uncertainties still remain the general history of firearms is well documented and the main lines of development are fairly easy to follow. The dates at which certain inventions, innovations and improvements were introduced can be identified fairly precisely and from the 17th century onwards many mechanical features are covered by written patents which give an exact dating. With this vast amount of information to hand it is usually not too difficult to date most firearms with reasonable accuracy. Certain national characteristics also evolved and these too enable a fairly clear provenance to be ascribed to most firearms. Unfortunately the same cannot be said for edged weapons.

Basically edged weapons are very simple and consist merely of a blade and a hilt and the number of possible variations on these, the combination of guards and so on, is fairly limited and therefore it is not surprising that styles of design are found recurring at differing dates and in different places throughout the world. The history of swords is also, of course, much longer than that of firearms and, in consequence, the gaps in our knowledge, particularly for the earlier periods, are considerable and it is often difficult to be precise as to the provenance and date of any given sword or dagger.

One of the earliest materials used for cutting was, of course, flint which is a truly versatile mineral but is, none the less, subject to some severe limitations. To produce a sword in flint would tax the technical ability of even the most advanced flint knapper and even if such a weapon were produced the weight and balance would be very awkward. Secondly flint is very brittle and a hard knock would invariably shatter the weapon. Some early cultures overcame this problem by mounting flint flakes, which have surprisingly sharp edges, on to a wooden former or holder to produce a kind of 'saw-sword'. Flint daggers, spearheads and arrowheads have been produced in quantity throughout the whole of man's history and in some parts of the world production continues to this day. When the first Spanish invaders landed in America they found themselves opposed by warriors using flint headed arrows and flint edged swords and the pioneers of the American West, some three centuries later, similarly found themselves under attack from flint headed arrows.

With the development of a metal technology, man's capability to produce edged weapons was greatly enhanced. Copper, with its relatively low melting point and ease of casting and moulding, offered an ideal material for the production of long sword blades but it did have one inherent disadvantage in that it was rather soft. No matter how often the edge of a blade was sharpened hard usage resulted in chipping and blunting. When the early inventors discovered that a small amount of tin added to copper produced a much harder metal, bronze, they were able to overcome this problem to a certain extent. The number of bronze swords, spear heads and axe heads produced throughout the ancient world must have been very considerable indeed, judging by the comparatively large numbers that have survived. During the long Bronze Age smiths produced great numbers of blades varying in length, size, weight and shape. The most common would seem to have been the leaf shaped blade which widened gradually from the point and then tapered again before widening once more at the hilt. Most of the Bronze Age swords were cast with an extension at the top end of the blade known as the 'tang'. To this tang were secured two plates of horn or wood or possibly even leather, designed to afford a firm and comfortable grip for the warrior's hand.

The use of iron appears to have originated in Asia Minor and was probably a discovery of the Hittite culture. Knowledge of the use of iron spread slowly from the south east across Europe and its great advantages in strength and retention of an edge ensured that it replaced bronze as the prime material for sword blades. Many of the early Iron Age swords, quite naturally, repeated the shape of their predecessors of the Bronze Age. Unfortunately for posterity iron is subject to rust and the number of surviving examples of early Iron Age swords is comparatively small. Bronze was not discarded at once and the two materials continued in use side by side; bronze and copper were often used for decoration and metal fittings on scabbards were probably of bronze.

Our understanding of the history of swords begins to deepen from the time of the Ancient Greeks, and it is interesting that some of the earliest Greek swords discovered are essentially long, thin, thrusting swords but other examples from the Mycenean civilisation are of the more conventional, broad bladed, cutting swords. During much of Greek history the main burden if fighting was borne by the heavily armoured foot-soldier, the hoplite, whose principal weapon was a long spear. However most of the hoplites did carry a short, broad-bladed sword, not dissimilar to the later Roman example. The Greeks also produced a very efficient slashing sword, very similar in design to that of the Gurkha kukri. Known, probably, as a 'kopis', this sword was fitted with a fairly short, broad blade, which, unlike most swords, was not straight. It had a slight double curve and the cutting edge was on the inside of the curve so that the general shape and distribution of weight made it ideal for close-in slashing cuts.

The Romans, too, favoured the short sword although their main emphasis was on the use of the point rather than the edge. This problem of optimum use of a blade was to remain a bone of contention throughout the entire history of the sword. There were those who maintained that the prime purpose of the sword was to thrust and use the point, whilst others maintained that it was primarily a cutting or slashing weapon. Many efforts were made to produce a weapon which effectively allowed the use of both edge and point but, since in many cases the design requirements were directly in opposition, at best they were a compromise. The Roman *gladius*, carried by the foot-soldier of the Roman legions, was a fairly short, broad-bladed weapon tapering sharply towards the point. The grip was usually of bone or ivory and the sword was carried in a sheath which was suspended on the right-hand side of the soldier. This carrying on the right-hand side was made possible by the comparative shortness of the *gladius* for the scabbard could be tilted forward and the sword drawn with one easy movement. Generally speaking the Roman legion's plan of battle was to lay down a barrage of spears, the 'pilum', and to follow this with a charge of the well disciplined and highly trained legionaires. Towards the end of their Empire the Romans found themselves frequently fighting cavalry and since the cavalryman was raised well above the ground it follows that his sword must necessarily have had a longer blade if he was effectively to strike an enemy foot-soldier. The *spatha* was a long bladed sword, probably adopted from the Gauls and then introduced into the Roman cavalry.

The years following the fall of the Roman Empire were ones of constant warfare and it is during this period that the sword achieved a simplicity of design and an efficiency of purpose that was seldom equalled in later periods. The broad, double-edged blade, measuring between 30 to 36 inches in length, had but a rudimentary point and was intended primarily as a slashing weapon. In the event of an enemy's blade being parried and sliding along the edge some protection was given to the hand by a cross bar, the 'quillon'. The tang, made as an integral part of the blade, was fitted, usually, with a two piece, wooden grip and at the end of the tang was attached a heavy weight known as the 'pommel'. The sword, housed in a wooden sheath, often lined with wool to give a natural greasy protection against rust, was normally carried on the left. So proud were the owners of the keenness of their swords that many gave them names extolling their virtues and swordsmiths proclaimed to the world their pride in the quality of their products

79

by inlaying their names in copper along the blade.

Sword design was obviously controlled by its purpose and this, in turn, was defined by the means of attack. When the armourer was able to produce efficient body protection by the use of mail or plate armour, the swordsmith was forced to produce more efficient means of attack in the way of larger, heavier, sharper or specially designed blades. As the efficiency of armour increased so the need to deliver a heavier blow acquired greater importance. From the mid 13th century it became increasingly common for the swords to be made of such a size that they could be managed with a one-handed grip but there was sufficient room on the hilt to grasp it firmly with both hands to deliver a more effective blow. Since the swords of this period were primarily slashing weapons the blades were usually broad, double-edged and with only a slight taper towards the point. Again, probably as a result of improved armour, from the late 14th century certain swords were designed specially to be used, in effect, as a small lance to thrust at the less well protected parts of an enemy's anatomy. These had blades which were usually of fairly thick section either hexagonal or square.

Whilst the general shape of the sword remained but little altered during this period, in some cases the quillons were straight, in others they were slightly down-curved. Some evidence for dating is afforded by the pommel although it is difficult to be dogmatic about the shape. Generally speaking the earlier ones from the 10th and 11th centuries are those shaped rather like a rugby ball or the recumbent D. From the middle of the 12th century a round, wheel-shaped pommel became very common indeed. Earliest examples were simply a flat-sided disc but from the early 13th century the edges were bevelled and this bevel increased from the middle of the 13th century and the general thickness of the pommel was much greater. Some swords were fitted with triangular pommels from the mid 14th century and these continued in use until the late 15th century. Some were conical and from the 13th century onwards occasional globular or egg shaped pommels were found. Some further slight guidance is given by the quillons for the early examples dating from the 12th century are usually fairly short and thick and from the early 12th to the mid 14th century the majority of quillons were fairly straight and far thinner but from the third quarter of the 14th century some quillons were produced with tips which curved upwards. During the early part of the 15th century the *landsknechts*, mercenary troops from Germany, favoured a short, broad-bladed sword which had its own distinctive shaped quillons—S-shaped and curving strongly back on themselves.

The quillons, apart from offering some protection for the hand, also offered a means of obtaining a better grip and from a quite early period it appears to have been common practice to hook the forefinger over the quillons. This necessitated leaving the top inch or so of the blade unsharpened and this blunted section is known as the 'ricasso'. During the 14th century this method of hooking the finger over the quillon became very widespread and the ricasso is quite common from the mid 14th century. In order to guard this finger, which had now lost the protection of the quillon, extra bars were fitted to the hilt.

From the 16th century onwards a number of factors contributed towards a change in design; first a greater emphasis on the point encouraged the swordsmith to produce extra protection for the hands for a single cross quillon gives little protection against a thrust. Secondly the thrust called for a lighter, thinner blade often without any sharpened edge at all. It is from the beginning of the 16th century that the 'swept hilt' rapiers and 'cup hilt' rapiers had their origin. From the early 16th century onwards there was an increased interest in the method of sword fighting known as fence in which the point was of prime importance, and the exponents of the art spent hours practising various parries and thrusts, measures and countermeasures. Since the rapier was designed primarily for stabbing there were those who argued that the longer the blade the more effective the weapon and some 16th century rapiers of quite inordinate length were produced. A proclamation was made by Mary Tudor and Philip on 17th March 1557 stating that swords or rapiers should not be "above the length of a yard and a half quarter in the blade at the most". Duelling became commonplace although, in England, it never reached the almost epidemic proportions of France.

Enthusiasts for the new science of fencing developed auxiliary aids in their quest for improved techniques for many felt that the left arm and hand, which often served merely as a balance, could be better utilised. To it were fitted such devices as a mail-faced glove, used to grasp an opponents blade without risk of injury; a torch or lantern, presumably to blind an opponent, or a cloak wrapped around the arm to serve as a parrying device. Possibly the most popular of all was a short dagger with which the fencer parried an opponent's blade whilst attacking with his own rapier. For some reason this particular style of fencing was especially popular with the Spanish and remained in common use there long after the rest of Europe had abandoned it. Many of the rapiers and left-hand daggers, 'main gauche', were decorated en suite, that is with the same pattern repeated on both the sword and dagger hilts. The Spanish enthusiasts favoured a particular form of left-hand dagger which was very characteristic and easily identifiable, for it was fitted with very long, straight, narrow quillons and a triangular shaped guard which curved from the quillon up over the hand and back to engage with the pommel. The rest of Europe favoured a more conventional dagger with simple quillon and a ring extending sideways from the quillon block to afford some protection to the hand. Rapiers remained popular until roughly the middle of the 17th century when they were gradually replaced by a variety of swords known as the 'small-sword'.

The origin of this particular type of sword appears to have been France and it differed from the rapier in having a shorter blade and was fitted with a hilt which was far simpler than that of the cup or swept hilt rapier. The design was modified over the years and between roughly 1630 and 1780 the trend of design is reasonably clear. The hilts of most small-swords consist of a double shell guard surmounted by a quillon block from the top of which sprang two fairly short arms which swept gracefully round to meet the two shell guards. When the sword was held in the hand, the first and second fingers were slipped through these two loops formed by the arms of the hilt. The grips, widening towards the centre, were of wood and bound with wire, sometimes silver, sometimes copper or similar materials.

During the 18th century small-swords became as much articles of costume as weapons and, in consequence, the hilts were quite elaborately fashioned with carving, chiselling and some later examples were fitted with enamel grips. Despite their long life of a century, there are one or two features which can be of assistance when dating small-swords. On the early examples the shells are generally of unequal size; one to the left of knuckle bow usually being larger than that on the right, but this difference had largely disappeared by the early 18th century. The shells later tended to lose their appearance of being constructed of two separate pieces and became a comparatively flat, single, oval plate. Another clear dating feature is the size of the two rings, the arms of the hilt, which swept out from the top of the quillon block. As the style of fence changed the method of holding the sword was altered and these arms of the hilt, originally intended to accommodate the first two fingers, were reduced in size until, by the latter part of the 18th century, they were little more than vestigial.

Small-sword blades were of three main types; there were those of more or less conventional, flat oval section with a double edge; a lighter form known as 'hollow ground', which had the virtue of rigidity with minimum weight for the blade was of a triangular section but with the side of the triangle ground well away to give a star like appearance to the blade. A third, and very distinctive, form of blade was the 'colichemarde', traditionally named after Count Königsmark, an adventurer of the 18th century. The top section of this form of blade is very broad but there is a pronounced constriction about a third of the way along from the hilt so that the rest of the blade is quite narrow. The virtues claimed for this design were strength and rigidity at the 'forte' (the top part of the blade) but a light thrusting section permitting swift movement.

Although the wearing of swords in Britain was generally abandoned around the 1770/80s, certain civic dignitaries retained theirs as a symbol of office and the present day diplomatic sword is, in effect, a very debased form of the 18th century broadsword.

Whilst the rapier and the small-sword might be quite decorative and, for their period, expensive; the ordinary man who felt the necessity of carrying some form of personal defence, found them far too costly and he would have favoured a short sword of the type usually known as a 'hanger'. These vary quite considerably but most were fitted with a single-edged blade which, on the examples of the late 17th and early 18th centuries, were almost invariably slightly curved. The hilt was simple with a grip of stagshorn, a knuckle bow and a small, down-curving, rear quillon; many had a shell fitted to the left hand side of the quillon. During the latter part of the 17th century and for most of the 18th century the hanger varied somewhat with the blade being more often straight and the hilt often dispensed with the side shell. This type of general purpose sword was very popular for hunting and many bear embossed decorations of hunting or classical scenes on the shell, knuckle bow and pommel. Many 18th century examples will be found in sheaths fitted with pockets to accommodate a knife and fork.

Whilst the hanger was convenient and light and the small sword was decorative and expensive, neither were really suitable for the hard rough wear of war and it was during the 17th century that the beginnings of regulation military swords can be discerned. During the greater part of the 16th century armies had been essentially collections of individuals and apart from such groups as the *Landsknechts*; few if any, members were issued with a uniform weapon. However, during the 17th century with the English Civil Wars, the Thirty Years War and the many other wars of succession and religion, the concept of a standing army gained ground. In Britain the armies of Cavaliers and Roundheads used very similar weapons including a type of sword favoured by the cavalry and usually known as a 'mortuary sword'. A long, straight blade was fitted with a hilt which consisted of a metal half-basket, a broad shell which was united with the pommel by several bars. Their name, 'mortuary', was given to these swords because so many of them bear a chiselled head which was claimed to represent Charles I although, in fact, it seems likely that the connection was nebulous to say the least. From the same period is the so-called 'Walloon' sword again with a straight, double-edged blade and a large spherical pommel, a single knuckle bow, small rear, down-curving quillon and, on either side of the hilt, two large rings which are usually fitted with a pierced plate. To afford a firmer grip a thumb ring extends across the right hand loop and shell.

Around the middle of the 16th century there first appeared the early form of the so-called 'basket hilted' sword. The term basket here refers to the cage or bars, straps and ribs which guarded the hand. Early origins are obscure but they probably originated in Germany. During the late 17th century many British Cavalry Units, particularly the heavy Dragoons were equipped with straight bladed swords which had a very distinctive basket formed by a squared mesh of metal bars. During the 17th century the Scottish broadsword seems to have acquired its characteristic form which, in some ways, is very similar to that of the Dragoon hilt. The Scottish sword has been known as a 'claymore' certainly since the 18th century although, in fact, this is an incorrect terminology. The word claymore is derived from *claidheamh mor* which means, literally, the great sword and refers to the long-bladed sword wielded in both hands by Highlanders of the 16th and 17th centuries. The true claymore had a very simple, cruciform style hilt sometimes fitted with a large defensive plate at the side to the centre of the quillon. The claymore is very similar in size and design to the large, two-handed swords favoured by the Germans and Swiss of the 16th century. These stood some 5 to 6 feet in length and many of them have a leather covered ricasso, the end of which is protected by two, downward pointing lugs which enabled the user safely to grasp the ricasso allowing the sword to be used as a shorter weapon. Some were made with a flamboyant blade in which the edges, instead of being straight, are marked off in a series of waves, the theory being that the curved edge gave much greater cutting power.

The two handed sword was largely abandoned by the 17th century and the spread of firearms was having an effect on the whole question of the value of swords as weapons. The pikemen whose prime job was to protect the musketeers whilst they were reloading, carried a sword and most of the cavalry of the period were similarly armed. The foot-soldier, also carried a hanger in addition to a plug bayonet.

Possibly because of its non-rusting qualities brass was a very popular material for the hilts of early military swords. Hangers with solid cast brass hilts incorporating lion head pommels date from the late 17th century, and around the middle of the 18th century most British infantrymen seem to have been equipped with a short, brass-hilted hanger which had a slightly curving blade and a simple cast brass hilt. Many of these swords dating from 1740–60 will be found bearing on the brass shell guard the identifying letters and numbers belonging to various county militia units. However, the bayonet and firearms were depriving the sword of any real functional value and in 1768 the British infantryman finally abandoned his sword; however the officer retained his and generally equipped himself at his own expense and taste. Most officers appear to have carried what is known as a 'spadroon', which was a robust, small sword type weapon. In 1786 a regulation was set down declaring that they should carry a sword of a certain type but unfortunately the regulation does not specify details. In 1796 another regulation sets down that the blade should be single edged, straight and the hilt was to be fitted with an urn shaped pommel and the grip bound with silver wire and fitted with a shell guard and small, stubby rear quillon. In 1803 yet another style of officer's sword was specified and this one was fitted with a curved blade and a quite elaborate style of multiple knuckle bow incorporating the royal cypher and, in certain cases, distinguishing marks for officers of flank companies. In 1822 a new style of sword was introduced for infantry officers and this style has a three barred guard which was formed from a knuckle bow which sprang from the pommel and split off into three separate bars curving round to make a very rudimentary basket. Eleven years later, in 1833, yet another novel form of sword, a mameluke type, was introduced and this was based, very loosely, on the shamshir, a sabre from the East. There was no basket at all and the single edged, curved blade was fitted with two short quillons; the grip of ivory terminated at the top in a right angled bend forming a type of simple pommel.

The next big change came in 1892 when, in place of the old Gothic style hilt, a sheet steel basket form of guard was introduced. This style forms the basis of the present day ceremonial sword carried by British Army officers. There were a number of variations of the pattern including having the designs embossed on the steel and many include a badge or emblem of the regiment.

Whilst the ordinary infantry soldier discarded his sword in the 18th century, the cavalry trooper continued to carry his until the cavalry were largely disbanded during the 1920s. As remarked above there was some dispute over the ideal sword for the cavalry and the two schools of cutting, slashing cavalry swords and stiff rigid, thrusting swords had their supporters. In 1796 a particularly attractive style of sword was introduced for light cavalry; this had a broad, slightly curved blade with a very simple hilt comprising a knuckle bow sweeping round from the pommel and a small, down-curving quillon at the rear, the form usually known as a 'stirrup hilt'. These were essentially slashing, cutting weapons and, in their steel scabbards, were carried by Hussars and Light Dragoons. For the heavy cavalry a straight-bladed sword with a flat disc guard was introduced and this saw service at Waterloo. In 1853 a sword for common use by light and heavy cavalry was introduced and this resembled, to some degree, the 1822 Gothic hilt of the infantry officers' swords. From the 1880s to the 1900s there was much discussion over the ideal sword for the cavalry and many committees made their reports which were either forgotten or failed to satisfy anybody until, in 1908, the results of the last committee were finally accepted. This report called for a narrow, rigid-bladed weapon with a large, cup-type guard and a specially shaped grip which, when held with fingers in the appropriate recesses, would automatically position the sword for a good, clean thrust given at the charge. In fact this sword was never put to a serious mass test under real battle conditions for the next major battle was, of course, World War I (1914–1918) during which only minor cavalry charges took place.

Naval swords were even more varied than those of the army until 1805, when an Admiralty order was sent out stipulating the official dress sword for members of His Majesty's Navy. The actual design varies according to the various ranks but the swords are less varied than those of the military. The 1805 pattern sword was fitted with a stirrup hilt and a straight blade and similar swords remained in use for several ranks for many years. In 1827 'half-basket' swords were introduced for some ranks.

Most naval swords incorporate somewhere in their design the fouled anchor, a naval symbol popular with many nations. It is an anchor of conventional design with a length of rope twined about shaft and flukes.

Naval and military swords will occasionally be found complete with their 'sword knots'. These were originally leather loops secured to the hilt and looped around the wrist to prevent accidental loss of the sword. The knots gradually became more elaborate and decorative and colours indicating the service were introduced, and the simple leather loop was replaced with tassels, bullion and fringes.

S.W.1. LEFT: Simple bronze dagger from Luristan, in Persia, dated about 1000 B.C.

S.W.2. RIGHT: Bronze Age sword with typical leaf shaped blade; two grips were fastened on the tang and the rivet holes can be seen on the shoulder.

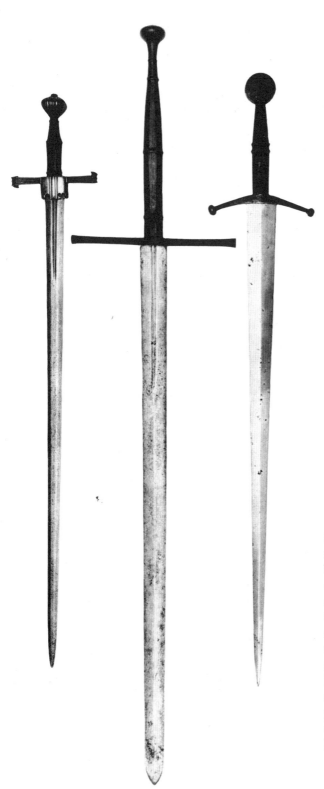

S.W.3. LEFT: German sword
of early 16th century with
bottle shaped grip, S-shaped
quillons and beneath a collar
covering mouth of scabbard.
Overall length 42 inches.
CENTRE: German two-handed
sword, 16th century with
straight quillons. Overall
length 55 inches. RIGHT: Hand
and half sword with flat disc
pommel and a slightly down
curving quillons. Overall
length 45 inches.

S.W.4.   LEFT: Mid-16th century rapier with blade of diamond section;
quillons and guards protected the hand and small hooks guarded the
finger hooked through to give a firmer grip.

S.W.5.   LEFT: Late 16th century two-handed sword with flamberge
blade. Overall length 79½ inches. RIGHT: Another similar date but with
straight blade bearing a spurious inscription

        ANNA DAMINE 1568 IN VOLENCZIA

Both have usual leather covered ricasso and cross lugs to guard hand.
Overall length 78 inches.

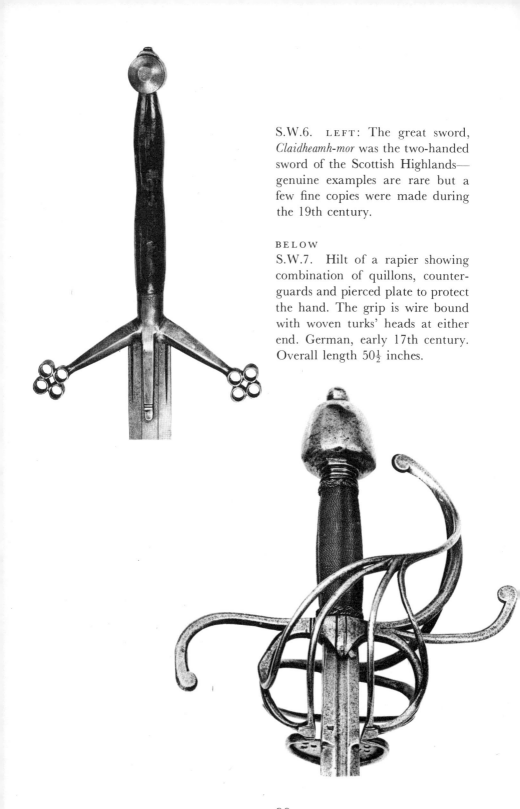

S.W.6. LEFT: The great sword, *Claidheamh-mor* was the two-handed sword of the Scottish Highlands— genuine examples are rare but a few fine copies were made during the 19th century.

BELOW
S.W.7. Hilt of a rapier showing combination of quillons, counter-guards and pierced plate to protect the hand. The grip is wire bound with woven turks' heads at either end. German, early 17th century. Overall length 50½ inches.

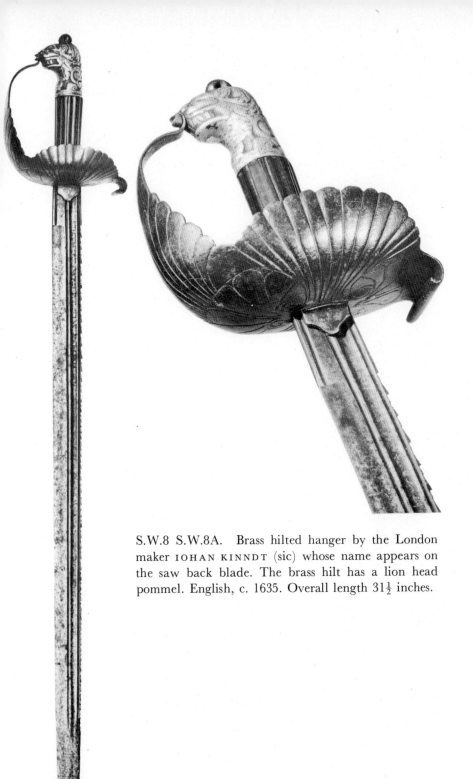

S.W.8 S.W.8A. Brass hilted hanger by the London maker IOHAN KINNDT (sic) whose name appears on the saw back blade. The brass hilt has a lion head pommel. English, c. 1635. Overall length 31½ inches.

S.W.9. Simple mortuary sword of mid-17th century with single-edged blade and bars secured to pommel by screws. On the blade are the names WELMM TESSCHE and WIERS BERCH. Blade 31 inches.

S.W.10. LEFT: Swept hilt rapier with loops and guards chiselled with foliage, c. 1600. Overall length 51 inches. CENTRE: Hilt encrusted with silver foliage and cherubs heads is quite a common style on English weapons of the early 17th century. The side rings are missing and the blade is later. RIGHT: Italian swept hilt rapier inscribed on blade ME, repeated three times. Late 16th century. Overall length 51 inches.

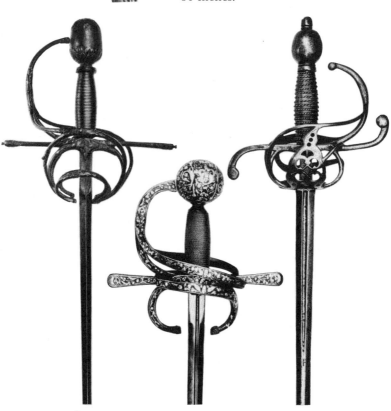

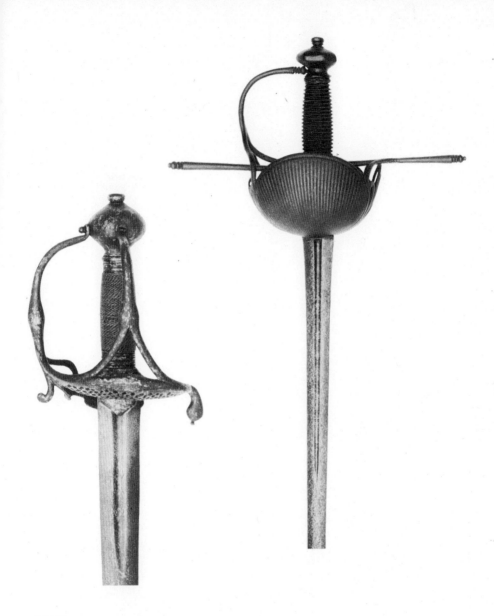

LEFT

S.W.11. Type of sword favoured by cavalry of the mid-17th century; 'Walloon' type although this is more ornate than most with gilding on the hilt. Overall length 39 inches.

RIGHT

S.W.12. Spanish cuphilt rapier of mid-17th century marked on blade ME FECIT SOLINGEN CONRATTI PRACH (grip replaced). Overall length $45\frac{1}{4}$ inches.

S.W.13. Small defence sword known as a pillow sword—made by IOHANNIS CONING of London. Traces of gold and silver inlay decoration on the quillons and pommel. English c. 1640. Overall length $28\frac{3}{4}$ inches.

S.W.14. Executioner's sword with double-edged blade bearing engraved legend VIM VIRE PELLERE LEGIT (It is lawful to meet force with force). Overall length 42 inches. Width of blade $2\frac{1}{4}$ inches.

S.W.15.   Spanish cup-hilt rapier and matching left-hand dagger. Overall
length Rapier 44 inches. Overall length Dagger 23 inches. Mid-17th
century.

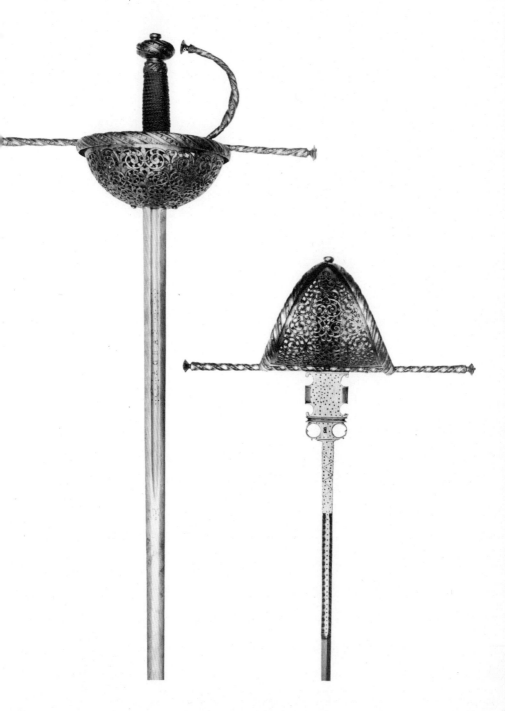

S.W.16. Hunting sword with sheath containing two small knives and a file; the horn grips are held by rivets with decorated heads. Dated 1662.

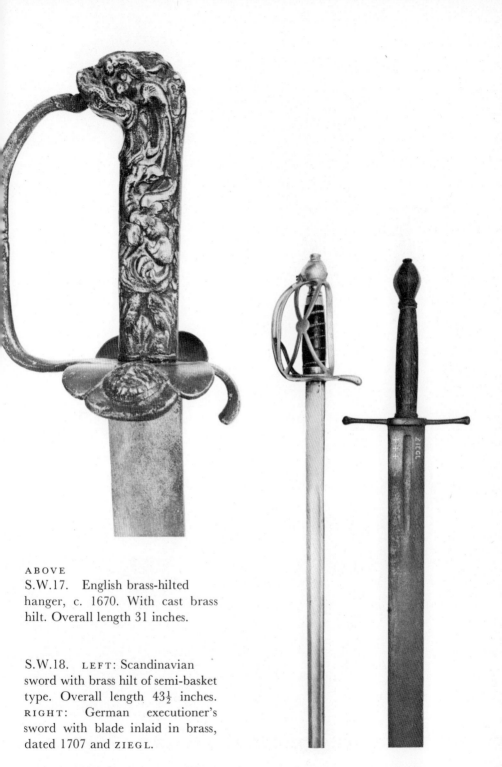

S.W.17. English brass-hilted
hanger, c. 1670. With cast brass
hilt. Overall length 31 inches.

S.W.18. LEFT: Scandinavian
sword with brass hilt of semi-basket
type. Overall length 43½ inches.
RIGHT: German executioner's
sword with blade inlaid in brass,
dated 1707 and ZIEGL.

S.W.19. Hilt of hunting
sword or hanger c. 1725. The
sheath is silver mounted and
on the locket is LOXHAM AT
YE ROYAL EXCHANGE.
Blade 25½ inches.

S.W.20. LEFT to RIGHT: 1, English hanger with silver plated lion's head pommel (c.f. S.W.8A) c. 1680. 2, Russian sabre with Turkish blade— hilt with eagle's head and the guard inscribed in Russian—For Bravery. Overall length 40¾ inches. Late 18th century, early 19th century. 3, spadroon, made for American market, gilt and blued blade with American motifs, made in Birmingham 1806. 4, Claymore with initials W. A. (Walter Allen of Stirling) under the guard and blade engraved ANDRIA FARARA. Mid-18th century. Overall length 38½ inches.

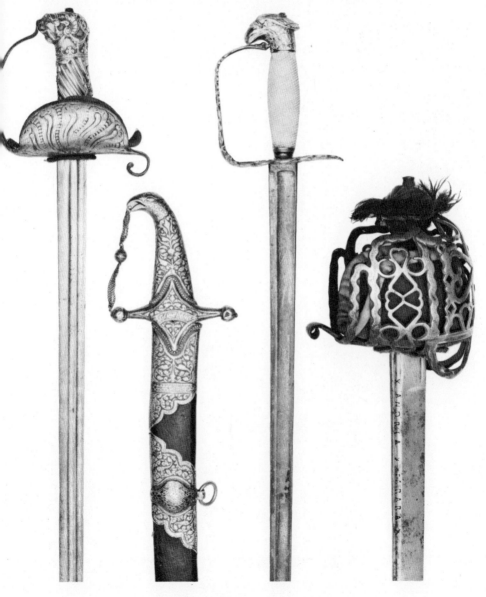

S.W.21.   1, Scottish broadsword with well decorated basket and blade. Signed ANDREA FARARA. Overall length 39¼ inches. Mid-18th century. 2, small-sword with silver hilt bearing marks for 1744 and maker's mark— John Carman. 3, combination sword pistol—brass guard and ebony grip enclosing the pistol mechanism. Overall length 27½ inches. c. 1770.

S.W.22.   Silver-hilted small-sword c. 1780 with grip bound with alternate silver wire and ribbon—hollow ground blade; pommel, guard and quillon block pierced.

S.W.23.   LEFT: Schiovanna, with steel basket and brass 'eared' pommel probably late 18th century. RIGHT: Italian swept-hilt rapier with guards embellished with blue glass in 19th century and ormolu borders and finials.

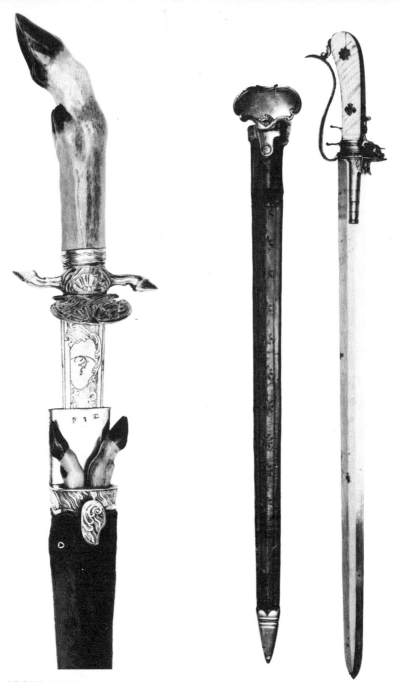

ABOVE LEFT

S.W.24. Hunting sword with Meissen porcelain hilts and silver marks for 1740. The two companion knives are similarly hilted. The hilts are fragile and presumably this was primarily a 'dress' weapon.

ABOVE RIGHT

S.W.25. Sword fitted with two pistols on either side of blade; the hilt is of ivory and grip strap is signed GUISEPPE AVERAN. The leather scabbard has steel mounts and a scallop at the locket protecting the flintlock mechanism. c. 1760.

S.W.26.   LEFT: French silver-hilted small-sword c. 1710, with triangular
blade inscribed HANNEBUFF SCHIEPO CAMIBUS PARIS. Overall length
37¾ inches.   RIGHT: Hunting sword with ivory grip, silver shell and
quillons and blade etched and gilt. The two glazed portraits on the blade
are probably of an Elector of the Holy Roman Empire and his wife.
Overall length 26½ inches. Mid-18th century.

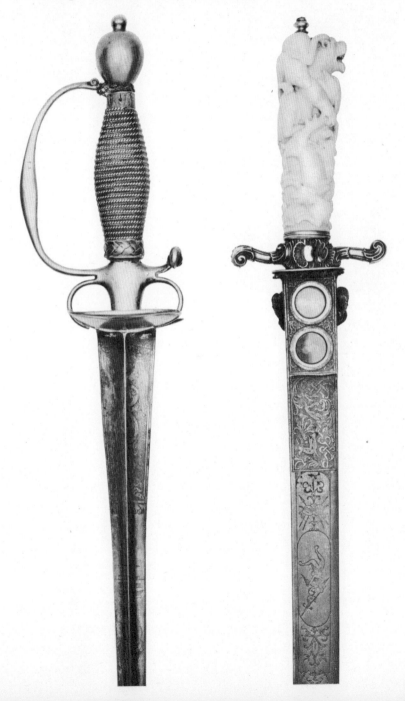

S.W.27. LEFT: German sword pistol with hilt of gilt brass and iron, downturned guard; the blade is etched and the pistol has been converted to percussion from flintlock. Overall length $32\frac{1}{2}$ inches. Mid-18th century. RIGHT: Early 18th century basket-hilted sword pistol—basket chiselled with dragon's heads and flowers. Overall length $28\frac{3}{4}$ inches.

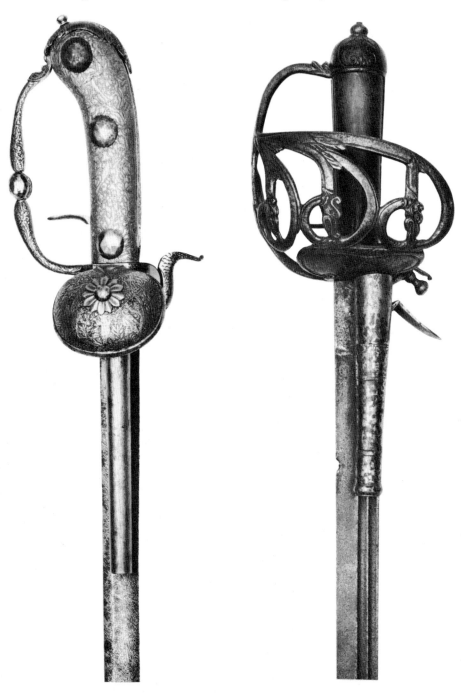

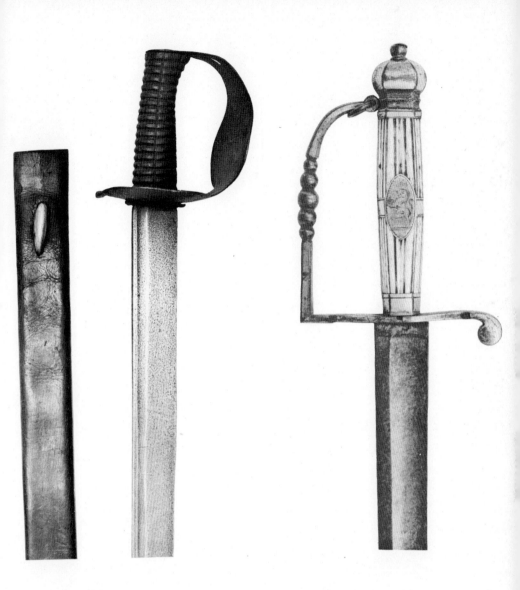

ABOVE LEFT
S.W.28.   British naval cutlass with double disc guard and ribbed iron grip. The blade is of the type used in the 1790s but the hilt is 1804 pattern. The black leather scabbard has brass fittings.

ABOVE RIGHT
S.W.29.   Officer's spadroon with typical five-ball hilt and pommel; the fluted ivory grip bears a cartouche of the arms of the Honourable East India Company. c. 1790.

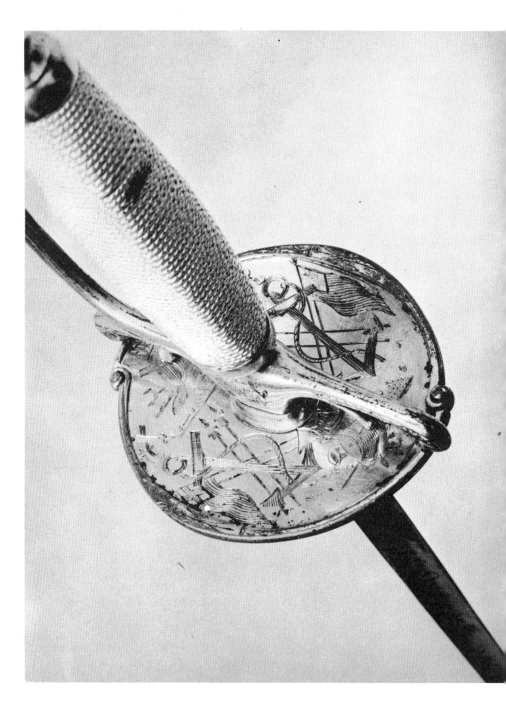

S.W.30. Shellguard of naval officer's small-sword. c. 1780—gilt with engraved naval trophies. Blade is blued and gilt. Overall length 34 inches.

S.W.31. S.W.32. Hunting swords with fluted ebony grips and steel fittings; the large-headed rivets are common on swords from Eastern Europe. Polish, 18th century.

S.W.33. Steel-hilted sma[l]
sword, c. 1730, pommel guar[d]
and shell all pierced, tr[i]
angular blade.

RIGHT: French revolutionar[y]
ceremonial sword with hilt [of]
gilded brass and scabbard [of]
gilt brass and red velve[t.]
This sword shows a stron[g]
classical influence and ma[y]
have belonged to a membe[r]
of the Committee of 50[0,]
c. 1800.

108

S.W.34. One of 18 £30 Lloyds Patriotic swords issued during the Napoleonic war—inscribed FROM THE PATRIOTIC FUND AT LLOYDS TO MR. JOHN GREEN MASTER MATE OF HMS GALATEA FOR HIS GALLANTRY AND PERSEVERANCE WHEN COMMANDING A BOAT BELONGING TO THAT SHIP IN BOARDING AND CARRYING THE FRENCH NATIONAL CORVETTE LYNX OF 16 GUNS & 161 MEN AS RECORDED IN THE LONDON GAZETTE OF 14 APR 1807.

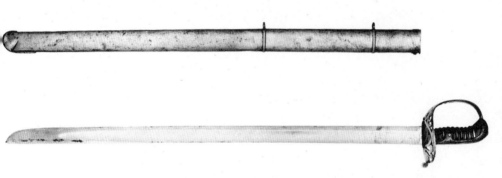

S.W.35. Heavy cavalry officer's sword with steel scabbard and wire-bound, sharkskin grip; the steel shell guard is pierced and resembles later patterns. 1796. Overall length 37¼ inches.

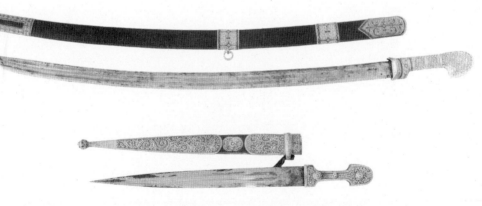

S.W.36. Cossack sword (shashqua) and dagger (kindjhal) decorated en suite with niello work and silver-gilt wire. Both blades are engraved in Russian ZLATOUST ARMOURY.

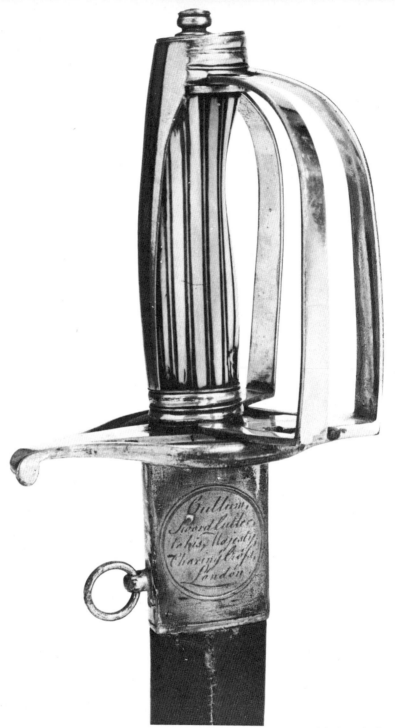

S.W.37. Sabre with ivory grip and gilt mounts, the knuckle bow is fixed but two pivoted guards swing out to form a half basket guard. Locket engraved CULLUM SWORD CUTLER TO HIS MAJESTY CHARING CROSS LONDON. C. 1800.

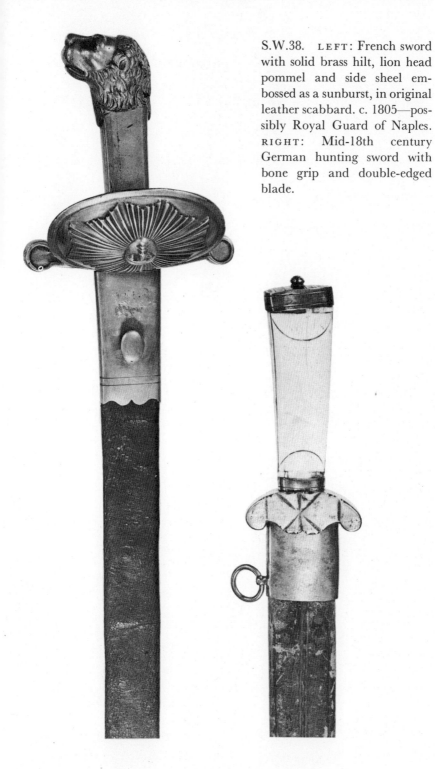

S.W.38. LEFT: French sword with solid brass hilt, lion head pommel and side sheel embossed as a sunburst, in original leather scabbard. c. 1805—possibly Royal Guard of Naples. RIGHT: Mid-18th century German hunting sword with bone grip and double-edged blade.

S.W.39. LEFT: Caucasian kindjhal with grip of black horn faced with silver—blade etched with Imperial eagle, scabbard with niello decoration. CENTRE: Dagger with ebony grip decorated with silver studs. Fluted silver quillons bear London marks for 1770. Overall length 13½ inches. RIGHT: Five ball hilted naval dirk with blade gilt and blue scabbard of leather with brass mount. c. 1800.

LEFT

S.W.40. Ornate hunting sword with chiselled decoration of crowned Belgian lions and classical figures on gilt copper hilt. Blade inscribed H.LE PAGE A PARIS MDCCCXXIX. Overall length 28½ inches. 1829.

ABOVE

S.W.40A. French heavy cavalry sword—straight blade with brass hilt and steel scabbard. The blade is 38 inches long and inscribed on back M F TURE IMPALE DU KLINGENTHAL 9 BRE 1813. This model was introduced in 1802–3.

S.W.41. Victoria umbrella sword with bone dog's head handle attached to blade $17\frac{1}{4}$ inches long and held in place by spring catch.

S.W.42. LEFT TO RIGHT: 1, Shasqua with silver-gilt hilt and niello decoration. 2, Shasqua with silver niello hilt and Arabic inscription giving date of 1911. 3, Shasqua with silver and gilt decoration. 4, Shasqua with large beak pommel and niello and gold filigree decoration.

S.W.43. Russian sword varying in detail from the 1909 officers' pattern, e.g. rear quillon is not pierced. Many Russian scabbards have the carrying ring on the front, the opposite of Western European practice.

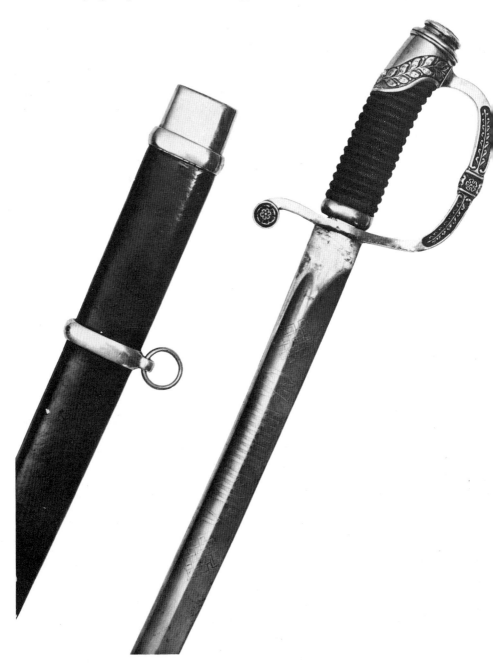

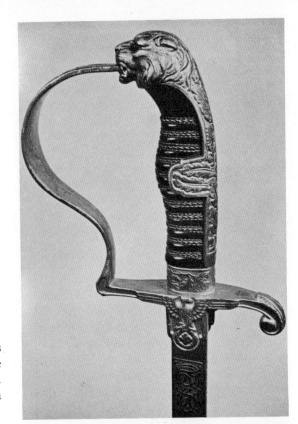

S.W.44. Nazi army officer's sword. The shape is basically the same as that of Imperial Officers. The eagle on the quillon holds a disc enclosing a swastika.

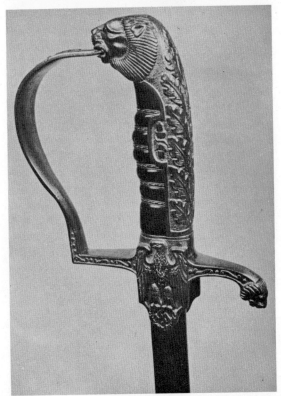

S.W.45. A variant of the Nazi army officer's sword, design patented by F. W. Holler of Solingen.

S.W.46. S.W.46A. Presenta
tion sword with gold inscrip
tion on blue background; gilt
brass hilt with side plate hinged
and the sword numbered No.
12. Silver wire bound grip and
blue leather scabbard. Overall
length 39 inches. c. 1940.
Inscription reads IN DANK-
BARER ANERKENNUNG DER
OBERBEFEHLSHABER DER
LUFTWAFFE HERMANN
GÖRING.

Small-bladed Weapons

The sword was usually regarded as the weapon of the nobility; a weapon of quality, whereas daggers and knives have been used by the ordinary people both as a weapon and a tool since time began. By definition a difference is made between a knife and a dagger although the distinction is often arbitrary; strictly speaking a dagger is double edged and has a tapering blade whilst a knife is single edged although some may have a small section of the back edge sharpened, referred to as a 'false edge'.

The earliest knives were, of course, of flint and were usually fashioned from a flake bound by some means into a wooden grip. Copper and bronze daggers were produced and the first iron daggers appear to date from about the year 3,000 B.C. and for some considerable period many daggers and knives were made with blades of iron but the hilts and fittings were of bronze. During most centuries the dagger or knife was essentially a reserve weapon and neither the Greeks nor the Romans appear to have placed much reliance on them as serious weapons. However, with the appearance of the Saxons and Vikings on the historical scene, the 'scramasax' or 'seax' became very common. These weapons were, by definition, essentially knives for they were single edged although some were fitted with a false edge. These knives were fitted with wooden or bone hilts and were produced in a wide range of sizes. Following the decline in importance of the Saxons and Vikings, the dagger somewhat fades from the military scene until about the 13th century when what was essentially a small version of the sword was in use. Known usually as 'quillon daggers' they were fitted with a single cross guard and a pommel not unlike those found on the sword. Appearing frequently on brasses of the Middle Ages is the rondel dagger which has a guard in the form of a solid disc and a pommel matching in shape and design the cross guard. The blades were fairly long and thin, often of triangular or square section. A rondel dagger was carried by the knights on the right hand side of the belt and was probably the dagger referred to in contemporary documents as a 'misericorde'. They appear to have continued in use until the early 16th century.

From the 13th to 16th century another peculiar, rather special type of dagger, known as the 'ear dagger', was in general use. They were found in France and England but appear to have originated in Spain. Their distinguishing features are two thickened disc projectiles which stand up at an angle from the pommel and this is what gives them their distinctive appearance and their name.

From the middle 16th century onwards there was a resurgence of interest in the dagger as the development of the rapier as an offensive weapon led to the introduction of the 'main gauche' or left-hand dagger, used, in conjunction with the rapier, to act as an auxiliary weapon of defence and attack. Most are of the quillon type with a fairly stout blade and quillons which curve down towards the point, often set slightly at an angle and with a ring mounted centrally on the quillon block. Both these features were designed to give some protection to the hand since the dagger was normally held with the blade uppermost so that the ring and quillons sat above the hand. Left-hand daggers were produced in a wide variety of forms. Some had serrated edges so that the blade could be used as a sword breaker, the idea being to catch an opponent's blade between the teeth on the blade and then, by a quick twist of the wrist, break the blade or at least disarm one's opponent. Others are made with blades of a cruciform section whilst others are pierced. As already mentioned above the Spanish produced a special form of left hand dagger with a very wide, triangular hand guard and long narrow quillon. These were certainly in use by the 1630s and continued to be used by the Spaniards until well into the 18th century.

Another very common type of late 16th and early 17th century dagger was the all-steel stiletto or 'stylet'. These were often turned from a single piece of steel and had a blade of square or triangular section and since they were intended primarily as stabbing weapons, had no cutting edge at all to speak of. The quillons were very short and stubby and the hilt was often of steel, sometimes carved and chiselled into fantastic shapes. Some of these weapons were modified to serve as a measuring device for the gunner in which case the blades were marked, or calibrated, with a series of lines and numbers. The numbering appears to be connected with the calibre of the cannon and the amount of powder used but, as yet, the exact correlation is not clear.

From the late 13th century right through until the 17th century, the form of dagger which was very popular had a fairly slim blade but a very characteristic hilt. The grip was usually of boxwood, although some were made of agate or metal; it was roughly cylindrical and fitted at the base with two large lobes which, in effect, formed stubby quillons. The distinctly phallic-like shape of the grip earned these weapons the name of 'ballock daggers'. The directness of this name offended some of the 19th century historians and catalogues and books of the period refer to them, rather disarmingly, as 'kidney daggers'. They were certainly very popular in England and examples will be found bearing inscriptions on the blades—some of which are distinctly earthy. It was this form of dagger which appears to have evolved into a characteristically Scottish form known as the 'dirk'. The two lobes at the base of the hilt were made bigger and also extended in length until they gradually assumed the characteristic shape seen on the Scottish dirk (see fig. E.D.6). The hilts are often decorated with Celtic scroll and interleaved strap work, whilst some of the more elaborate ones have the strap work embellished with the addition of silver headed nails. Although the later dirks were fitted with specially made blades they copied the appearance of the originals which were cut down sword blades. With the revival of Scottish romanticism in the early 19th century these dirks became very popular and many had large pieces of mineral, cairngorms, fitted on the pommel. They were housed in sheaths which also had pockets to hold a knife and fork decorated en suite with the dirk. Dress dirks worn by the various Scottish Regiments will be found to bear, naturally enough, the appropriate regimental badge.

For the ordinary person from the 17th century onwards daggers and knives became far less essential items of equipment but with the opening of the west of America in the 19th century the dagger and knife industry once again went into top gear for during this period there appeared, probably, the most famous knife of all, the so-called 'bowie' knife. This famous knife owes its origin to the Bowie family originally based in Maryland but which later moved to Georgia and then on to Tennessee and Louisiana. There were three brothers of which two are primarily concerned with this famous weapon; Rezin, who claimed to have produced the very first bowie knife, and his brother James who is more popularly associated with it. Rezin claimed that he first designed the knife in 1827 and that it consisted of a straight blade $9\frac{1}{4}$ inches long, $1\frac{1}{2}$ inches wide, with a single edge running right the way along to the guard. James Bowie lived an adventurous life; so adventurous that it is now virtually impossible to separate fact from fiction. He eventually met his death in the rather futile battle of the Alamo in March 1836 and the romantic aspect of this event encouraged the growth of a myth and soon bowie knives were popular throughout the whole of America. Many were produced in America, but Sheffield, England's cutlery town, was not slow to realise the potential market and, in fact, the vast majority of American bowie knives were manufactured in England. Firms, such as Wostenholm and Joseph Rodgers & Son, soon began to exploit the market by producing a great variety of weapons, often with suitably etched mottoes proclaiming for death or liberty, or exalting the Union.

121

Exactly what constitutes a bowie knife in present day terms is difficult to say but the majority of collectors would probably describe it as a knife with a single-edged blade with a large, clipped, false edge. The hilt, made of wood, brass or mother of pearl, was normally fitted with a small cross guard or two stubby quillons. Most bowies were originally carried in a leather sheath with metal chape and locket. One popular variety of this knife had a silver horse head pommel.

Another very popular knife produced during the 19th century was the Spanish 'navaja' which was essentially a large, folding, clasp knife. Some are of quite considerable dimensions and most have a straight blade with a large, clipped, false edge and when opened out it is locked automatically into position. There is often a spring fitted with a ring on the back which provides purchase when releasing the spring to allow the blade to fold back into the grip.

The next main stimulus to the renewed output of knives and daggers was the advent of Adolf Hitler's Third Reich. Germany had for long been one of the main arsenals of Europe and towns like Solingen had been famous for the quality of their sword blades for centuries. Following their defeat in World War I the German economy was in a parlous state and towns such as Solingen which had relied almost exclusively on arms production, found their unemployment situation catastrophic. With the upsurge of optimism subsequent to Adolf Hitler's take-over of power in 1933, the swordsmiths of Solingen sent a deputation to see the Fuehrer and suggested to him that it would be advantageous to the town, beneficial to the party and stimulating to the members if the Nazi regime would encourage the use of dress daggers and swords. Anxious, no doubt, to encourage the martial spirit of their followers the Nazi leaders readily agreed to this proposition. Suggestions for appropriate designs were sought and the first model accepted was based on the so-called 'Holbein dagger'. These were originally produced during the 16th century, with a fairly short, broad blade tapering gracefully to a point and a grip which was rather like a capital letter I. The sheaths were of gilt bronze or silver fixed to a wooden base and Hans Holbein, the artist, produced the design for one of these sheaths; for which reason they have become known as Holbein daggers. The Nazis accepted this version and it was first issued to the S.A., the Sturm Abteilungen, in February 1934. The sheath was in metal, quite simple in design and brown in colour and the wooden hilt of the dagger matched the colour of the sheath. Set into the wooden grip was a stylised S.A. and the blade was etched with an appropriate patriotic motto *Alles für Deutsch-*

land. Naturally the S.A. was not alone in demanding daggers and variations for the Black Squad, the Schutzstaffeln or S.S. were soon produced; these differed in that the wooden hilt and the sheath were black and the blade carried a different motto *Mein Ehre Heist Treue.* Soon other units, political and military, were demanding daggers and the Army, Navy and Air Force had their own variations although theirs were of a more conventional type. Customs Officials, Air Raid Wardens, Water Police, Emergency Squads, Flying Squads and Transport Corps all had their own version of a dagger and many officials also had swords.

One form of edged weapons which has retained its military usefulness over the last three hundred years, is the bayonet. Its origin lies in the difficulties encountered by early musketeers who found that once they had discharged their musket they were defenceless and encumbered with a large, useless weapon. Some protection was afforded by pikemen but this was wasteful of manpower and made for formations which were distinctly cumbersome in use. Sometime during the second quarter of the 17th century there originated an idea of converting the empty musket into a form of pike and this was done by pushing into the barrel a long bladed knife. Bayonne in Southern France, was famous for the quality of its hunting knives and it is this town which gave its name to this new use for a dagger or knife, the bayonet. At first they were simply long daggers with a round, plain wooden hilt, fitted with a simple cross guard, although others had more elaborate cast, brass guards. The hilt was rammed firmly into the muzzle and did indeed convert the musket into a seven-foot pike but it had one serious disadvantage for when in position in the muzzle this type of bayonet rendered the musket useless as a firearm. Efforts were made to overcome this by fitting the bayonet to the outside of the barrel and the first attempts were made using rings which were secured to the wooden grip and slipped over the barrel. This simple form of attachment was later replaced by the 'socket' bayonet which had, in place of a wooden hilt, a short length of metal tube which was appropriately sized so that it could slip over the muzzle of the musket. In order to secure it firmly a slot was cut which could engage with a lug mounted on the tip of the muzzle; by this means the musket could still be loaded and even fired with the bayonet in position. These socket bayonets were to remain in general use until well on into the 19th century. Blades were normally triangular in section and mounted on a short, curved neck so as to take them well clear of the muzzle. In order to prevent the accidental loss, or even the deliberate pulling off of the bayonet, some were fitted with spring clips which helped to hold them firmly in position. During the 18th and 19th centuries many efforts were made to produce a bayonet which could also serve as either a tool or a sword and many of these had quillons, knuckle bows, saw edges and other features which quite often defeated their original purpose. One big improvement was in the method of attachment and the new system used a lug and socket arrangement whereby the hilt of the bayonet was slotted to engage with a lug mounted usually on the bottom of the barrel and the quillon was broadened and cut with a circular hole which slipped over the muzzle. When placed in position the channel in the back of the hilt engaged with the lug on the base of the barrel and the circular, cut-away quillon slipped over the muzzle and a spring clip locked the bayonet firmly into position. This style of fitting, with variations, has remained in use until the present. During the 19th century a great variety of bayonets were produced both in Britain and on the Continent and some of the more unusual are highly sought after by modern collectors. The 'jacob' bayonet was produced for a double barrelled rifle and was one of the longest ever to be used by the British, thirty six inches overall, and when in position on the end of the barrel its length and weight must have made the weapon most unwieldy. It was fitted with a large, cut-away guard in the style of the British Infantry officer's sword.

Around the middle of the 19th century it became very popular to fit bayonets with 'yataghan' type blades which had a double curve; certainly Enfield rifles had such a bayonet as did some of the French models. In 1873, during the Ashanti campaign, Lord Elcho introduced a special type of bayonet which had a very broad blade which widened to some considerable degree and was intended to serve as a machete for clearing a way through the jungles of the Gold Coast.

During World War I the design of the bayonet became more or less standard with a short, wooden grip, a straight blade of varying lengths and, at best, a fairly short cross guard or quillon. World War II, with the introduction of many automatic or repeating weapons, saw a general reduction in size of bayonets and a far more utility look was developed, some being little more than spikes or knitting needles stuck on the end of the rifle. A few weapons, such as the Russian sub-machine gun, were fitted with a spring operated bayonet which was permanently attached to the gun.

E.D.1. LEFT TO RIGHT: 1, Italian stiletto with triangular blade. Early 17th century. 2, left-hand dagger with pierced quillons and pommel, overall length $16\frac{3}{4}$ inches. Late 16th century. 3, ballock dagger with wood grip and iron pommel, overall length $14\frac{1}{2}$ inches. Late 16th century. 4, rondel dagger but with replacement grip, overall length $20\frac{1}{4}$ inches. Late 14th century.

E.D.2. LEFT TO RIGHT: 1, left-hand dagger—Italian. Overall length 16 inches. Mid-16th century. 2, early 17th century Saxon dagger from Dresden Armoury with silver gilt plaques set in pommel and quillons. 3, Italian ear dagger, overall length $11\frac{1}{4}$ inches. Early 16th century.

ABOVE LEFT

E.D.3.   LEFT to RIGHT: 1, French rondel dagger, overall length $13\frac{1}{4}$ inches. Mid-15th century. 2, ballock dagger of 16th century. 3, English dagger with silver decoration on hilt, overall length $12\frac{1}{4}$ inches. Early 17th century. 4, Italian stiletto with chiselled hilt, overall length $11\frac{7}{8}$ inches. Early 17th century.

MIDDLE

E.D.4.   17th century stiletto with turned wooden grip and diamond section blade—small steel quillons extend from central block. Blade $10\frac{1}{4}$ inches.

RIGHT

E.D.5.   Peasant dagger with wooden grip carved like a woman and a back edge blade engraved DI PICF FRANCESCO PAOLI with false edge. Overall length $16\frac{1}{4}$ inches. 17th century.

E.D.6. Dress dirks of 71st Highland Light Infantry. 1, made by Meyer
and Mortimer of Edinburgh. Hilt carved with typical strap work set with
cairngorm. Sheath still has fork in pocket. c. 1860. 2, made in Glasgow by
Leckie Graham & Co., sheath with regimental badge, knife and fork.
c. 1890. 3, silver-plated mounts, knife and fork.

E.D.7. Presentation dagger in silver, sheath inscribed THIS KNIFE WAS USED BY HIS EXCELLENCY SIR RICHARD TEMPLE GCSI GOVERNOR OF BOMBAY AT THE UNVEILING OF THE STATUE OF HIS ROYAL HIGHNESS THE PRINCE OF WALES PRESENTED BY SIR ALBERT SASSOON CSI KT TO THE CITY OF BOMBAY JUNE 26TH 1879.

E.D.8. Unusual steel knife which locked onto a special shaft to form a spear, engraved BALDOCK KNIFE SPEAR MADE EXPRESSLY FOR WALTER LOCKE & CO. LTD PATENTED and on the opposite side JAMES DIXON & SONS SHEFFIELD ENGLAND. Overall length $13\frac{3}{4}$ inches, blade $9\frac{1}{4}$ inches. Mid-19th century.

E.D.9. Bowie knives of mid-19th century including fine example with horse's head pommel.

E.D.10. English and American knives of late 19th century—all of English origin, except fourth from left from New York.

E.D.11. Caucasian kindjhal embossed and decorated with niello work. The blade, 13½ inches long, is double edged and has a long needle point.

E.D.12. Spanish navajas with long, characteristic blades. Most of these have spring operated catches to lock the blade in open position and hilts in various materials.

E.D.13. Silver-mounted knife and sheath from the Argentine. Popular all over South America as a general purpose knife as well as a weapon. Overall length 17 inches.

E.D.14. During the 3rd Reich daggers were worn by many officials apart from those of the armed services. This was the German Customs Service model and has a green covered sheath to match the grip.

E.D.15. A seemingly ordinary pocket knife, really a World War II German paratrooper's knife with a heavy blade dropping into position when a catch is released.

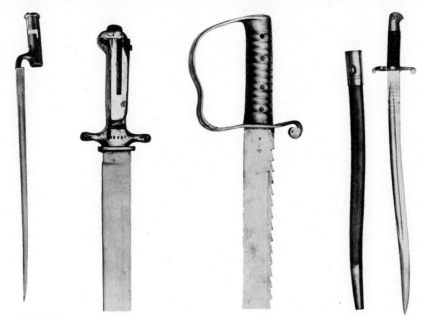

B.1.   Socket bayonets replaced plug bayonets early in the 18th century and have remained in common use until the present. This is for Brown Bess, India Pattern, musket. Overall length $21\frac{1}{4}$ inches. c. 1800.

B.2.   LEFT: Prussian hirschfanger, a solid brass hilted bayonet, blade $18\frac{3}{8}$ inches. RIGHT: Brass hilted sword issued to Pioneers; 1856 pattern, withdrawn in 1903 and re-issued to Royal Navy as cutlasses. The saw-back enabled the sword to be used as a tool. Overall length 27 inches.

B.3.   Yataghan bayonet for Enfield percussion rifle—it locks to barrel by a slot which engages with a lug on the barrel while muzzle passes through hole in quillon. Black leather scabbard with steel fittings. Overall length 28 inches. Blade $22\frac{3}{4}$ inches.

B.4.   Hilt of bayonet for the Jacobs double-barrelled rifle. The longest bayonet ever issued to British forces, measuring 36 inches overall.

131

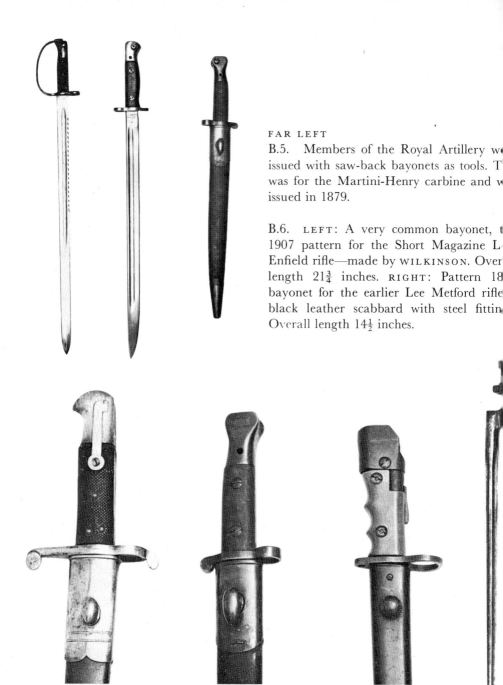

FAR LEFT
B.5. Members of the Royal Artillery w
issued with saw-back bayonets as tools. T
was for the Martini-Henry carbine and w
issued in 1879.

B.6. LEFT: A very common bayonet, t
1907 pattern for the Short Magazine L
Enfield rifle—made by WILKINSON. Over
length 21¾ inches. RIGHT: Pattern 18
bayonet for the earlier Lee Metford rifle
black leather scabbard with steel fittin
Overall length 14½ inches.

B.7. LEFT: Hilt of B.3 showing spring clip which engaged with barrel
lug. CENTRE: Hilt of B.6 (right) showing similar clip at very top.
RIGHT: Hilt of Mk. 7 bayonet designed to fit both the Mark 4 Lee-
Enfield rifle and the Sten gun. The grips are plastic.

RIGHT
B.8. Russian socket bayonet, model 1891, which saw use in both World
Wars. It had a cruciform section blade and its flat point was used for a
screwdriver.

Weapons from
the East

That the East should be so often described as colourful is hardly surprising; bright sunlight, dark shadows, extremes of riches and poverty and a harsh struggle for life, may well have produced a rather special view of life and beauty. These same factors have probably influenced the attitude of mind concerning war, for most of the weapons from the Middle East, Asia and parts of the Far East, are far more decorative than their European equivalents. It may be that the resultant ornate and sometimes rather bizarre appearance of many Oriental weapons has discouraged European collectors from showing much interest. One exception to this generalisation must be made with the swords of Japan which have been popular with collectors for many years; they are also different in that they are simple, severe and technically excellent and can often be identified and dated precisely.

Over the past few years there has been a gradual change in attitude on the part of collectors and this has been the result of a number of factors. Certainly availability has been a very important factor for the price of European items has risen so sharply that for many collectors, it has become impossible to afford them and consequently many have turned to cheaper fields of collecting including Oriental weapons. More information has become available in the form of reliable books and these have obviously stimulated interest. There has also been an increase in the number of good quality items on the market and this has been one of the unforeseen results of the ending of the British Raj. Many Indian princes were forced, by circumstances, to review their financial position and as many had maintained arsenals of all manner of weapons for centuries, the possibility of converting these assets to cash was soon appreciated. Many of the arsenals of India have been stripped of most of their contents and many of these have found their way to Britain to such an extent that it is probably easier to find good quality pieces of Indian craftsmanship here than in India itself.

It is almost impossible to detail the development of Asiatic weapons in a short chapter such as this and the best that one can do is to offer some general guidance in the nomenclature and design of some of the weapons.

India

The sub-continent of India has a long, martial tradition and within its borders many cultures have met, combined and diverged but each has left their mark on weapon design. Not only were there many native cultures but India was, from the 15th century, subjected to European influence, first by the Portuguese and later by the French and British, whose cultures also made their impact on weapon design.

Generally speaking the Indian warrior was a swordsman and as an auxiliary he naturally made use of a shield, and circular Indian shields—'dahl'—are fairly common. They are often to be found made of some hard, natural material such as rhinoceros or buffalo hide, in which case they are often treated to give a semi-transparent appearance, or they are decorated with painting. Many are made from steel, often with a brass rim, and this type is frequently covered with chiselled decoration. There is a third type which is of hide covered with a layer of thick lacquer. One common feature to all these shields, no matter which type, are the four small bosses mounted on the front. These are normally the fittings by which the means of holding the shield were attached to the back, usually two straps passing from the top to the bottom boss. Between the straps was placed a well padded cushion which broke the force of any blow taken on the shield.

The majority of Indian swords are known as 'talwars' although, in fact, this is merely an Indian word for sword. Talwars vary in shape of blade and style of hilt and the collector is referred to Rawson's THE INDIAN SWORD and Stone's GLOSSARY OF WEAPONS for details. The most common types have a disc pommel, a grip that widens at the centre and, usually, a guard of two stubby quillons. Some but not all, have a curving knuckle bow springing from the front quillon and meeting the disc pommel. Most talwars are of all metal construction including grip and most have two short 'langets', bars which extend from the base of the hilt, and hold the sword firmly in the scabbard. The blade can be straight or curved in either direction and most are single edged. Sheaths are usually of wood covered with velvet or leather and many have twin leather thongs at the top which were used to tie the sword firmly in the scabbard. Some talwars have decorative chiselling on the blades and, in general, these are primarily ritual or sacrificial weapons.

Pommels of a similar shape to those on talwars are also found on swords with straight, double-edged blades and these are known as *firangi* (foreigner) since the blades were usually of European origin. Another sword with a long, double-edged blade, but with a strengthening rib along part of the back edge, is the 'khandar' but this type differs in having a basket type guard. The pommels on most khandars have an extension which was intended to give purchase if a double handed grip was required.

Peculiar to India was the 'patah' often described by collectors as a 'gauntlet sword' since the grip was by means of a metal glove-like guard fitted with a cross-bar. The hand was slipped inside the guard and the bar gripped so that the blade projected forward rather like a lance; it was primarily a horseman's weapon.

From India, Persia and surrounding countries comes the 'shamshir' which again will be found in a variety of forms. although most have a single edged, curved blade, two short quillons and straight grip with a short pommel set at right angles to the grip. Some shamshirs and similar sabres have such pronounced curves that the back of the scabbard is split in order that the blade may be withdrawn.

Knives and daggers were so common in India that there are numerous examples of every quality and design still to be found today. Distinctive and easily recognised is the 'katar', a punch dagger, with its stiff, triangular blade and an H-shaped hilt which is gripped by the cross-bar. More often decorative with hilts of jade are the 'khanjars' which usually have curved blades. Larger and simpler is the 'Khyber' knife with a long, straight, acutely pointed blade and a simple, straight hilt with a slightly over-curving pommel. One feature of these weapons is the way in which they sit in the scabbard so that only the tip of the pommel is visible above the mouth. Straight bladed, but smaller, are the 'kards' which often have a thickened tip designed to permit easy piercing of mail. This feature will be found on many Asiatic daggers and knives.

One type of dagger found over wide areas of India, Persia and the Middle East, is the 'jambiyah'. The only feature which can be said to distinguish this type of dagger is the acutely angled blade. The hilt varies according to the place of origin; those from India and Persia are usually flat topped whereas those from the Middle East have large pommels either semi-circular or fan shaped.

From Nepal comes one of the commonest of weapons, the Gurkha's kukri with its heavy, curved blade sharpened on the inside edge of the curve. The sheath usually has two small pockets which hold two implements, a small skinning knife and a sharpening tool.

Axes figure prominently in the Indian armoury, some being extremely ornate with hooks and blades of sinuous shape. Maces were often fitted with long hafts and a hilt very much like a khandar.

Indo-Persian firearms are, like the edged weapons, often highly decorative and examples using any one of the three main forms of ignition; match, flint and percussion, will be found. Quality varies from distinctly crude to superb. Matchlocks are quite common and are usually of the type classed as a 'torador' which has a long, almost straight, stock and a forward moving serpentine which is usually housed mainly within the stock. Barrels are secured to the stock by a series of bands which may be of rawhide or strips of brass. Another type, a very distinctive form, is the 'jezail' which has a very strongly curved butt, the so-called 'Afghan' stock although, in fact, ir originated in the northern part of India, the Scinde. On muskets from Persia, the Caucasus and Turkey the stocks tend to be far more chunky and solid and are frequently inlaid with horn, semi-precious stones and other decorative materials; some even have tassels and velvet coverings on the stock. Pistols are less common although Indian gunsmiths did produce a few which used a matchlock, including some which had a number of barrels to produce a simple, repeating weapon.

Burma, Malaysia and Indonesia

The characteristic weapon from Burma is the 'dha' which, in a superficial way, resembles the Japanese sword, being slightly curved and usually plain or with only simple decoration. The grip of wood is cylindrical and lacks any form of guard; the sheath may be silver mounted and fitted with a thick, tasselled carrying cord. North, in Assam, live the Nagas and their characteristic weapon is a halberd-like axe called a 'dao'. The head is flat and frequently has a V-shaped recess cut into the front edge.

From Malaya and the many islands of Indonesia comes the 'kris' with which is associated much folklore and a certain amount of controversy. This weapon will be found with straight or sinuous blades but the distinguishing feature is the grip which is fitted at right angles to the blade so that the weapon can only be used with a thrusting motion. Identification of origin is based on the differences in shape—those from Malaysia have sheaths with a square top, those from Bali are rather more oval, whilst those from Java have a graceful, upswept, prow-like top section. The Malaya kris usually have a very acutely angled grip but Javanese tend to be almost straight. Blades of these weapons are normally greyish and have a very rough textured surface which encourages some enthusiastic, but ill-informed collectors, to polish them smooth so destroying one of their original features. Some larger versions of the kris with more conventional, smooth textured blades, were used by the sea-dyaks and these are called 'sundangs'.

136

Oceania

From the numerous islands spread across the great Pacific Ocean the most common weapon is the club and these were little valued up to a few years ago but as interest in ethnography grew so did the demand until now rarer examples, such as those from the Marquesa Islands, fetch a figure in excess of £150. Identification is not always easy and reliable sources are scarce. Clubs with a grip very similar to that of a sword can usually be ascribed to New Guinea, whilst a peculiar boat-shaped type is from Santa Cruz Islands. Elaborate and detailed carving covering most of the surface was a feature of the work of Fijian wood carvers and the same craftsmen produced a style of club which resembles the outline shape of a musket.

China and Japan

Although superficially linked in so many ways, China and Japan differ so much in the quality of their weapons. China may have given the world gunpowder, printing and other inventions but, perhaps to her credit, the quality of weapons is generally fairly low, whereas Japanese swordsmiths were among the most skilled in the world, indeed many would claim that they were never equalled.

Japanese swords differ in so many respects from those of Europe; the traditional approach of the smith ensured that the shape and design remained practically unaltered for centuries. It is difficult to date these weapons on general appearance but, for the expert, there are subtle indications of age. The blade is of supreme importance and normally has a slight curve and is single edged. There are three sizes of sword—the largest being the 'tachi' and 'katana', with blades over 2 feet long. The former was worn on certain occasions and was carried in a sheath which was suspended from a girdle whereas with ordinary dress a katana was worn and this had a plain sheath which was pushed through the girdle. Since the Japanese warrior class, the Samurai, carried a pair of swords known as 'daisho', a second, shorter sword accompanied the longer blade. With the tachi he wore a 'tanto' which had a blade around 10–11 inches long, but unlike the large sword it had no guard. The pair to the katana was a 'wakizashi', which was simply a smaller version of the larger sword. The hilts of wood were covered with a layer of rough fish skin known as 'same' and this was bound with a layer of silk braid and on both sides of the hilt, under the braid, was placed a tiny, metal ornament, usually finely decorated, known as the 'menuki'. The flat guard, 'tsuba', was of metal and decorated with any one of a series of techniques or combinations thereof, including inlay with precious metals, lacquer and chiselling. Most of the smaller swords have the sheath adapted to hold two extra tools—a long. thin knife, the 'kodzuka' and a skewer-like device, used by the warrior to dress his hair, the 'kogai'.

The appraisal of a Japanese sword is a matter of some complexity and the tyro will need to read as much as possible and look at as many examples as possible before he can hope to get any understanding of the finer points.

In addition to the swords the Japanese produced a number of polearms and the quality of the blades is generally very good and again they are simple in design, whereas the Chinese and Burmese examples are usually ornate, not to say faintly ridiculous.

Japanese firearms are almost invariably matchlocks, for following their initial contact with the Portuguese they closed their towns and minds to western influence, and it was not until the mid-19th century that European ideas impinged on them. As a consequence firearms design stagnated for three centuries and then leapt into the 19th century so that wheel-lock, snaphaunce and flintlock were passed over and their next step was directly to percussion and cartridge weapons. The matchlocks are generally of good construction with simple but tasteful inlay on the barrel and some embellishment to the stock. Two distinguishing features are the weight of the barrels which are usually very thick and heavy and the use of brass for the construction of the springs resulting in a slightly soggy action.

Examples of miniature Japanese weapons and armour will be encountered and these are not toys in the general sense but rather small copies made for the Boys' Festival when examples of weapons were displayed outside the houses.

Weapons from the East

O.D.1. Asiatic weapons were often very ornate with applied decoration; this 18th century dagger from India has gold inlay and rubies on the jade hilt and a 6-inch blued blade. Over 40 jewels, rubies and emeralds are fixed to the leather covered scabbard.

O.D.2. LEFT: Katars, known as punch daggers from their style of use, were popular in India. This has a maroon coloured sheath and gold damascening on the hilt. RIGHT: Unusual set of straight bladed daggers, kards, which fit inside each other, all have ivory grips and damascened foliage decoration on the blade.

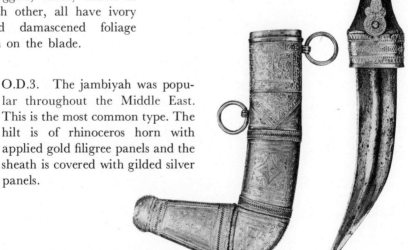

O.D.3. The jambiyah was popular throughout the Middle East. This is the most common type. The hilt is of rhinoceros horn with applied gold filigree panels and the sheath is covered with gilded silver panels.

O.D.4. Persian khanfar with damascened
blade reinforced at the point and a hilt of
nephrite carved with foliage. The wooden
scabbard is covered with material with metal
mounts. Overall length 16¾ inches. 18th
century.

O.D.5. LEFT: Persian dagger with gold
damascened blade and ivory hilt embellished
with carved scrolls, leaves and flowers. Overall
length 14¼ inches. Early 17th century.
RIGHT: Unusual nephrite talwar hilt of
common form with gold inlay and spaces to
hold precious stones. This superb hilt is fitted
with a cut-down small sword blade. Overall
length 21 inches, hilt 6 inches. Late 18th
century.

O.S.1. LEFT: Japanese military sword known as Kaju-gunto, with two handed grip and gilt brass hilt fittings. A compromise between traditional Japanese and Western styles. RIGHT: A firangi from India with unusual two handed grip. The hilts are steel with engraved brass and the grips are covered with cloth; blade double edged.

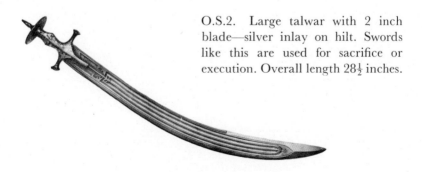

O.S.2. Large talwar with 2 inch blade—silver inlay on hilt. Swords like this are used for sacrifice or execution. Overall length 28½ inches.

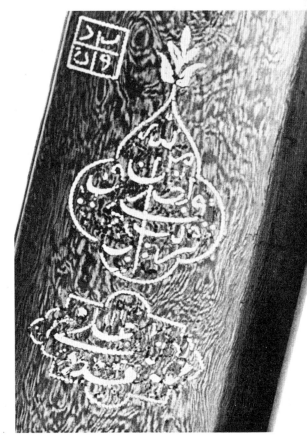

TOP LEFT
O.S.3. Conventional Malayan kris and sheath. The sheath is made from three separate differently coloured woods; the blade is sinuous, fitted with a carved wooden grip in stylised bird form. Overall length 14½ inches.

TOP RIGHT
O.S.4. Detail of a talwar blade showing texture of metal and inlaid cartouches of gold with inscription invoking Allah and Alli. The small quartered square is a lucky talisman.

LEFT
O.S.5. LEFT: Early Indian steel sword with short grip and hole for finger. CENTRE: Talwar with steel pistol grip, ball pommel and quillons each fitted with a folding blade. All three blades have separate scabbards. RIGHT: All metal sword possibly from Tanjore with two jingling pieces fitted to pommel.

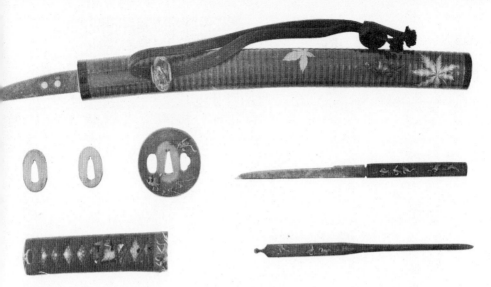

O.S.6. Tanto stripped down to component parts. TOP: The blade inside the scabbard shows two holes in the tang. CENTRE: Left the two washers—seppa—which fit at top and bottom of the tsuba, the circular guard. The knife which goes in a slot in the scabbard is called a kodzuka. BOTTOM: The grip and the kogai which fits into the scabbard.

O.S.7. Finely decorated fittings from top and bottom of a Japanese sword hilt, the kashira and fuchi and a fine iron tsuba chiselled with details of the tea ceremony.

O.S.8. Long Japanese sword tachi scabbard with gold overlay TOKUGAWA, family badge or mon. All fittings of shakudo engraved with tendrils. The 29 inch long blade signed on the tang YAMASHIRO KAMI HIDETOKI.

O.S.9. LEFT: Parrying rod—Hachiwar—with square section blade 13 inches long, with hook just below the guard. The hilt is mounted like a conventional sword but hung from the body by the blue cord. CENTRE: Aikuchi of very good quality with fittings in gold and silver; the lacquered sheath has some silver mounts and the extra knives are also present. RIGHT: Tanto—lacking tsuba but well decorated with gold foliage patterns; the sheath is burgundy red in colour and with applied gold lacquer decoration.

Armour

From the first day that man took up a weapon it was inevitable that another man would seek to provide some means of defence and this contest between the armourer and the weapon maker has continued right up until the present. It is useless to speculate on the nature of the very first defence but it was probably some form of shield and it is not unreasonable to assume by analogy with present day primitives that it was fashioned from wood and was little more than a shaped piece of trunk or branch with a hand-hold cut at the back. Details of early shields are sketchy and as the majority were made of wood their chances of survival were very small. On rare occasions a 'pavise', as used by archers of the Middle Ages to protect themselves whilst loosing their arrows, does turn up in the sales rooms. The only other likely examples are the rare 16th century parade shield or an occasional small, steel Tudor buckler which is a simple, circular shield sometimes with a hook or spike at the centre.

The majority of shields that the collector is likely to see, will almost certainly be ethnographic. Commonest of all are those from India which have already been described above, followed by those from the Sudan and North Africa. These shields are made of buffalo or hippopotamus hide and are normally round with a central boss, the inside of which is spanned by a strong bar by which the shield is held. Numbers of these were brought back to Britain after the Sudanese campaigns in the late 19th century. The majority of Zulu shields, which are larger and oval with a long thin stick traversing the length and passing through a number of slits in the hide, are tourist pieces although authentic ones are occasionally found. Shields, frequently fashioned from a single piece of wood, that are flat with a hand grip at the rear, are likely to be of Dyak origin. Similar ones which may be of wood, buffalo hide or even woven wicker and decorated with clumps of coloured hair, are likely to be those of the Nagas of Assam. for these people favour this style of decoration on shields and weapons. One of the most ornate types of shield comes from Ethiopia and although they are similar in shape to those from the Sudan they are far more elaborate, being covered overall with a fine silverwork, sometimes in the form of patterns, sometimes simply an odd arrangement of stripes and circles.

Effective though the shield was, it was not without its limitations, especially as one hand was fully occupied in holding it and this could be a great handicap. It also offered only partial protection being of little use against the unexpected attack. What was needed was some form of body defence that was permanently in position and required no holding, leaving both hands free for action.

The first piece of real armour of which we have evidence is the helmet; although its exact date of construction in the Assyrian culture of the second millenium B.C. is open to speculation. By the first millenium the Assyrians, a notable warrior race, are depicted as wearing some form of protective cape which was probably of leather reinforced with some form of bronze rings. From this simple form of defence it was a fairly direct step to the production of 'scale' armour whereby the body was protected by a series of overlapping metal plates secured to a basic garment. Scale armour remained a popular form of body defence for many many centuries and it was used by almost every culture in the Middle East as well as the early Greeks. Examples of Mycenaen scale armour have been excavated and there is also some evidence for a form of soft armour made of folded linen.

The Greeks took the next logical step in the development of armour and increased the size of the scales, eventually turning them into large plates which were shaped to the body. The Greeks also produced several styles of superb helmets, the 'Corinthian' type is the one most people think of as being Greek, it was of bronze and covered the head completely except for a T shaped opening leaving the nose and eyes clear. The Greeks also produced some extremely fine plate armour in the form of a 'cuirass', that is breast and back plate, and armour for the lower part of the legs, known as 'greaves'.

When Rome first established her supremacy in Italy the Roman legionary was probably protected by a coat of mail known as the *lorica hamata*. Where the Romans gained the knowledge to make their mail is not known, its first recorded appearance seems to be in the second century B.C. The Romans referred to it as 'Gallic mail' so that it may be that they took the idea from the Celts although others argue for an Asiatic origin. The legionary's head was protected by a bronze helmet which was rather like a jockey cap with the peak at the back whilst the side of the face was protected by wide cheek pieces which were tied beneath the chin. The legionary carried a tall, rectangular shield which was curved horizontally to afford maximum protection. His main hand weapons were a short sword, the *gladius*, and the throwing spear, the *pilum*. During the first century A.D. the Romans changed much of their equipment and in place of the old mail shirt they were equipped with the *lorica segmentata*. This was a superbly designed set of plates, made in four sections, two of which crossed the shoulder to protect the upper part of the body and hooked on to the other sections of curved lames which were laced up at the front. When not required the *lorica segmentata* was collapsed into a neat little packet which could be placed in the legionary's bag and suspended from a pole carried over his shoulder; the total weight was around 12 pounds. This form of Roman armour continued in use until the third century A.D. Also during the first century A.D., in place of the fairly simple bronze helmet, the legionary wore an iron helmet with a much wider spreading neck guard, large cheek pieces and a reinforcing bar which fitted across the brow. On the top of the helmet was fitted a holder for a crest.

After the passing of the Roman Empire there are many gaps in our knowledge of the history of armour but it seems that the Vikings and Saxons leaders and nobles relied on mail. The ordinary foot-soldier probably depended almost exclusively on a simple, round shield, which had a central boss covering the hole into which the hand fitted when holding the bar.

Mail was to continue as the main form of body defence for many centuries and was not really abandoned until the 17th century. Very few examples of European mail dating prior to the 15th century have survived and indeed most pieces of mail encountered will almost certainly be of Asiatic or African origin. Indian and Sudanese mail was produced in quantity and most of the mail shirts seen in antique shops are of 19th century Sudanese origin. One reasonable guide as to origin, although not necessarily infallible, is to examine the links; European mail was almost invariably of riveted construction each ring having the ends flattened and riveted together. Mail from Asia and Africa has the rings 'butted', that is bent round so that the ends merely touch, being held there by the rigidity of the metal.

Mail was a very efficient means of body defence but it had its limitations. Basically the only way to increase its defensive quality was to thicken the links but this made the mail far less flexible and much heavier. Its defensive qualities were greatest against the slash or cut, but against the thrust of a pointed missile such as an arrow or the point of a lance or pike, it was far less effective. In seeking to increase defences the armourer was forced to examine alternative means and the method he adopted was to reinforce the mail with small metal plates. The first positive verification of this use of extra plates occurs around the middle of the 13th century when small shaped plates, 'poleyns', were fitted at the knee. Similar extra defences were fitted at the elbows and these were known as 'couters'. Once the principle of using plates had been developed it was not long before plates, sometimes quite crudely shaped, were being fitted on the arms and legs. There are also references to a 'coat of plates' and this was a surcoat with a number of metal plates riveted on the inside; these were very popular during the 14th century. In the 14th century there also appeared plate neck defences and by the second quarter of this century complete arm defences were fairly common. Beneath the plates the knight was still wearing a coat of mail, the 'hauberk'. By the early 15th century the armourer's skill and technical knowledge had advanced sufficiently to enable him to produce a complete body defence of plate. Armour of this period is extremely rare but sufficient examples have survived to show the skill with which the armourer fashioned his product. Thickness of the metal is graduated so that at the points of maximum danger the plate is thicker gradually shading off to the less vulnerable areas. The armour was secured to the person of the knight by means of leather laces known as 'points', which were attached to an arming doublet. This was a carefully padded garment with patches of mail sewn on at vulnerable points such as the inside of the elbow, underneath the armpit and at the groin. The documentation of armour of this period is quite extensive for there are numerous brasses, illuminated manuscripts, engravings and miniature paintings, all of which show the armour in some detail, although actual specimens are very rare.

Around the middle of the 15th century there evolved one of the most attractive styles of armour ever produced and this is known by collectors of today as the Gothic form. Generally speaking the characteristics of this armour were the graceful fluting and scalloped edges; the breast plates were of two pieces to allow for ease of movement and from the base of the breastplate hung a narrow skirt of lames. Many of the main plates were edged with a thin strip of brass. Small pieces of Gothic armour do occasionally appear in the sales rooms but their rarity ensures that they fetch a high price even if in poor condition. Italian armour of the same period tends to be far smoother in outline and less spiky in appearance. During the 15th century, armour styles changed but it had reached its ultimate form; for external events such as the general adoption of gunpowder and the evolution of fresh tactics were rendering armour obsolete. However, during the early part of the 16th century a style of armour which was rather a compromise between the German and Italian styles appeared and this is usually referred to as being 'Maximilian'. Generally speaking the outline is rounder and more Italian but the entire surface, except for the greaves, was covered by lines of fluting which gave strength and rigidity to the pieces. Much of the armour of this period is characterised by the so-called 'roped edge' where the end of the metal was rolled over and then marked with a series of oblique lines to give the appearance of a piece of twisted rope.

From about the 1530s the style of breastplate changed somewhat and they became flatter and then began to develop a central ridge so that by the 1580s this central ridge had become very pronounced and, in fact, terminated at the waist with a distinct pointed projection resembling the civilian fashion known as 'peascod'. During the early part of the 16th century there appeared the 'black and white' armours which were fairly simple but the surface was covered with a fairly thick layer of black paint leaving only a border, an inch or so wide, which was polished bright. These black and white armours are not uncommon and usually consist of a breast and back plate; from the breast plate was suspended a series of 'lames', or plates, which extend down to cover the thighs as far as the knees. Shoulders and neck are protected by a further series of lames forming a collar known as a 'monnion'. The armour is completed by the addition of two gauntlets.

The abandoning of armour was accelerated during the 17th century and by the time of the English Civil Wars it had been severely reduced in quality. Cavalrymen had a breast and back plate and one or possibly two elbow gauntlets which were padded and fitted at the top with a loop so that they could be tied to the arm. The musketeer had by now abandoned all armour, a few retained a helmet but the majority went into battle armourless. To protect them from attacks by cavalry during the period that they were loading their muskets, the musketeers had blocks of pikemen who were still armoured. They wore a fairly substantial breastplate to which was attached a wide, flaring skirt of tassets, fairly bulky and made in one piece although decorated to look as if constructed of a series of lames. The backplate was far thinner and lighter. Many cavalrymen and many foot troopers also wore a buff coat, an ironical return to the earliest form of armour. These thick leather coats were sufficient to turn aside the edge of a sword although insufficiently strong to deflect a bullet, but they offered protection without restricting too much the movements of the wearer. By the end of the 17th century only a few cavalry units in the British army retained their breast and back plates and these were largely abandoned early in the 18th century. For most of the 18th century armour was primarily a matter of academic interest although many of the notables felt it had martial significance for they obviously liked to have their portraits painted showing them in full armour.

During the 19th century there was a revival of interest; in Britain in 1821, the Household Cavalry were once again fitted out with breast and back plate and a metal helmet. Although the breast plate was fairly substantial, the helmet was essentially a decorative piece since the metal used in its construction was quite thin. The French continued to favour the use of armour and at Waterloo and early in World War I the heavy cavalry of the French army differed but little in appearance, still wearing steel helmets fitted with high brass combs and fur crests as well as heavy breast and back plates.

During the numerous wars of the 19th century desultory experiments in the use of armour were carried out and there are authenticated records of its use during the American Civil War and the Franco-Prussian war. During the first World War there was a great deal of interest in forms of body protection and both British and German armourers experimented in the production of body armour. The most common type which turns up is that made by the Germans for their machine-gun crews and snipers and consists of a quite substantial breastplate with tassets protecting the thigh and a reinforcing piece which fits on to the brow of the helmet.

Although, broadly speaking, armour was abandoned in Europe by the 17th century its use in the East continued until comparatively recent times and in India, Persia, Turkey, Japan and Africa, armour of various forms was worn until this century. In India padded armour was very popular and the picturesquely named 'coat of a thousand nails' was very much like the European 'jack' or 'brigandine' in that the basic garment was reinforced with rivets or small plates. The plate armour of India is basically of two styles; the fitting of plates to the padded garment and the 'coat of four mirrors' or *char aina* which is a cuirass made up of four separate plates, one for the front, one for the back and one for each side of the body. These plates are often decorated and fitted with brass edges. Persia was famous for its armour production with a tradition extending back through the ages. The Persian armours were commonly of the *char aina* type with the arms protected by sections of plate not dissimilar to those of Europe. These arm guards were usually fitted with a fabric lining and also had a mail glove attached. In Turkey there was a preference for a body defence comprising a mixture of plate and mail and the basic elements comprise a disc covering the chest which is usually fluted radially and connected to the main mail shirt. This form of body defence was very popular with Janissaries who formed the Christian born but Moslem trained bodyguard of the Turkish rulers.

In Japan a very different system of armour was evolved. The earliest examples appear to have been constructed of plates but during the 5th and 6th centuries A.D. the Japanese seem to have reverted to a form of lamellar construction using a series of small metal plates, usually lacquered, and laced one to another in rows or fastened to a basic garment. The body defences were made up of a series of large units of this lamellar armour with the cuirass of more conventional form, often just a large plate. Japanese armours were decorated and they are usually embellished with coloured laces and different lacquered materials on the plate. The style of Japanese armour did alter somewhat over the years but basically the late and early Japanese armours are superficially the same. As with Japanese swords the study of Japanese armour is a very specialised one and needs to be approached with caution by the enthusiast. Some of the pieces, such as the face masks which were intended to give a ferocious appearance to the warrior as well as offering some facial defence, are collected in their own right as individual pieces.

Helmets

Helmets were one of the very first pieces of armour and they are depicted on Assyrian sculptures dating back to 3000 B.C. However, apart from some highly decorative and ceremonial examples, few specimens of very early helmets have survived. It is with Classical Greece that the history of the helmet becomes clearer with the preservation in museums of numerous examples of superb Greek helmets. Many of these are marvellous examples of the armourer's skill, the entire skull being beaten from one piece of metal. Roman helmets too have survived and there are one or two examples of Saxon and Viking helmets. From the 11th to the 15th century our knowledge is drawn largely from documentary sources. The helmets are depicted on illuminated manuscripts, monumental effigies, monumental brasses and sculptures of the period but actual examples are extremely rare.

By the time of the Norman conquest the basic European helmet comprised a conical skull with a single bar, the 'nasal', projecting down to guard the face against a slash. During the next two centuries the armourer experimented with methods of improving the defence for the head and this he did by fitting various guards for the neck and the sides of the head and expanded the nasal to unite with the cheek and neckguards to form a tubular, barrel-like helmet which was eventually to become the 'great helm'. The shape of these helmets varied somewhat, some have a conical skull and a few even seem to have regressed in that the top of the helmet is made flat, a feature which diminishes the efficiency of the helmet since the deflecting qualities of a glancing surface are lost. The great helm became so large that the bottom edge of it actually rested on the shoulders, the inside was padded and the helm was held to the head by laces which were tied under the chin. It is hardly surprising that this heavy and cumbersome helmet was later replaced by lighter models. The great helm was essentially a cavalryman's armour and many foot-soldiers, and indeed some of the knights, favoured a war hat, the *chapel-de-fer*, which was much lighter. This usually had a conventional, rounded skull and was fitted with a wide, normally down-sloping brim but varying in detail.

During the 14th century occur the first mentions of the 'basinet', a term which was, in fact, applied to a number of helmets of differing pattern. The most common type was a helmet which reached down almost to the shoulders but with a large opening which left the face clear. To the rim of this helmet was attached a curtain of mail, the 'camail' or 'aventail', secured by passing a thong through a series of staples. When in battle the face was protected by a movable guard known as the visor which was fitted with two slits to allow for sight and a number of ventilation holes which afforded the wearer with a limited amount of fresh air. Many of the visors were attached by a hinge to the brow and these helmets are known by the German title of *klappviser*, others had the visor attached at both sides of the skull with a pivoted hinge. The pin of the hinge could be removed to allow the visor to be taken off completely. During the 14th century the bascinet began to displace the great helm as the most common form although the great helm was reserved for use at tournaments.

Towards the end of the 14th century a new style of helmet appears, the 'sallet', but again this is a blanket term used for a number of different styles. The most usual form of German sallet has a skull which is continued down to cover the face with only a wide slit for vision. At the back the skull was shaped to form a pointed tail which was sometimes long enough to be fashioned from several lames.

During the early part of the 15th century the 'armet' was developed and this was to set the basic form for most helmets for the next century or so. The armet consisted of a skull which had a narrow tail extending down the back of the neck. Fitted on both sides of the skull were shaped metal plates, hinged at the top. To put the helmet on these plates were lifted up and the helmet placed in position. The side plates were then lowered and locked in position so that the head was completely enclosed in a case of steel except for an open space allowing vision. A pivoted visor was fitted and this could be lowered to protect the eyes. Similar in appearance, but differing in construction, was the close helmet which first appeared very early in the 16th century. The close helmet differs from the armet in that, in place of the hinged cheek pieces a single, shaped guard, the 'bevor', was pivoted at the side and lifted to allow the helmet to be placed on the head and then swung down and locked into position leaving a quite large facial opening. This facial opening could also be protected by means of a visor and this was pivoted at the same point as the bevor. Close helmets were produced in a variety of styles; some were fluted in the Maximilian style with visors scalloped like a bellows, others of the latter part of the 16th century differed in the shape of visors and style of decoration. Some of those in the 17th century had a visor which was made up of grill-like plate and some, known as 'Savoyard' or 'Todenkopf', had a grotesque resemblance to a skull.

The close helmet saw a great deal of service during the 16th century but towards the end of this period lighter forms of helmet were desired and one of the first to appear was the 'burgonet'. This was an open faced helmet with the skull extending down to cover the back of the neck and with two cheek pieces which could be raised when putting on the helmet. Extra protection for the face was given by a peak which, on the early examples, was pivoted in much the same way as the visor. Again many of the earlier burgonets were made with an extra face guard, known as the 'buffe', which could be strapped on converting the burgonet back into a close helmet. During the second quarter of the 17th century a simpler form of burgonet was introduced with a rounded skull, a laminated neck guard which swept down and widened towards the base, two ear flaps, a fixed peak and with protection for the face provided by a sliding nasal bar. This was the type popular during the Thirty Years War and the English Civil Wars. The English version differed in that the peak was pivoted and the face guard consisted of a grill made up of three heavy bars and secured to the peak. For the foot-soldier the kettle hat remained quite popular although the brim was made far narrower and this type of helmet was often fitted with a comb on the crown and is usually described as a 'morion'.

From the mid-17th century onwards most infantry may be said to have discarded metal helmets completely. Some of the cavalry units retained them but metal helmets were out of fashion. Towards the latter part of the 18th century there was some experimentation with some form of head defence although often this was little more than a thick leather helmet. For certain climates leather was found to be unsuitable and thin, almost tin-plate, helmets were produced, some strengthening being given by the use of crests and so on. The French heavy cavalry undertook some developments in this field of helmets, fitting their heavy dragoons with steel skulled helmets decorated with bands of animal skin, brass combs, feathers and plumes of various kinds.

The general development during the 19th century was towards decoration rather than defence and most of the helmets of that period are of very thin brass or white metal and from their very nature were obviously intended primarily as decorative pieces. Some can only be described as ridiculous and the poor trooper or cavalryman who was supposed to wear them whilst going into action must have the sympathy of every early armourer.

The situation changed dramatically with the advent of World War I. When the war of movement of 1914 gave way to the war of the trenches of 1915 the most vulnerable part of the majority of combatants was their head which was exposed to all manner of bombardment from above. Early in 1915 the French began experimenting with light-metal helmets to reduce the number of head wounds. In June of that year they began issuing their soldiers with a metal helmet which consisted of a crown with a brim welded on and a central comb. A few months later the British developed their own style fashioned from one piece and basically very simple with a domed crown and narrow, slightly downward sloping brim. In late 1915 the Germans began to develop their characteristic *stahlhelm* which was to give such excellent service throughout two world wars. All these helmets were made with detachable liners; that is paddings and head fittings which were adjustable or adaptable to various sizes. Experimentation in this field has continued and is still being pursued using plastics and other new materials, the results of which have led to new patterns and new styles of helmets. There was an interesting return to the use of mail during World War I for tank crews were issued with a protective face guard which consisted of a leather covered metal mask with a curtain of mail attached at the base to cover the rest of the face. The idea was to protect the wearer against a spray of metal caused by bullets which shattered against the outside of the tank.

Helmets from the East have not varied in design anything like the same as those from Europe and those worn in the last few centuries in Persia, Turkey and India all have a strong superficial resemblance. Examples have survived from the 15th century in Turkey which are of the type known as 'Turban' helmets; they are very large and at the front have two small recesses cut to accommodate the eyes. Later metal helmets from these areas consist of a small crown, usually slightly conical and almost invariably fitted with a curtain of mail. On the Indian ones this mail curtain can be very short but the Persian and Turkish ones tend to have a far longer curtain. Most helmets are fitted with a sliding nasal bar although there is a difference in the method of securing this bar. Generally those of Indian origin have a hook and hasp to hold the bar in position whilst those from Persia more closely resemble the European model, having a threaded screw which can be set to hold the bar in position. Yet another difference between the two helmets is in the depth of the crown for, generally, and it must be emphasised that these are generalisations, the Indian ones are much shallower than those from Persia and Turkey. One type of Persian helmet often picturesquely described as a 'devil' helmet, has a grotesque face and horns on the bowl. These highly decorative types are usually of very late origin and are primarily for parade rather than fighting. The majority of these are fitted with plume holders in the form of narrow, conical sockets. Persian helmets usually have two fitted at the brow and at the top of the crown is a spike, whereas the Indian helmet tends to have three plume holders, two at the brow and one at the crown. Many types of decoration will be found on these helmets, sometimes they are covered with low relief chiselling of religious and Koranic inscriptions; some from India may well be inlaid with silver, brass or gold, usually in repetitive patterns.

In Japan helmets, like armour, took on a different form of construction and many are made up of a large number of thin plates arranged so that the edges project on the outside of the skull. The number of plates varied but often exceeded sixty. Generally speaking helmets of this type are of two parts, there is the skull of these plates, the top centre having a hole which was designed to take the queue of hair of the samurai warrior. A short peak is fitted at the front whilst the neck is guarded by a series of strips of lamellar defence, each one usually brightly coloured. On either side of the skull many of these helmets have an upward sweeping and backward curving lame known as the 'fukigayeshi'. At the front of the helmet there is a slot which held the support of some form of crest which might be wide horns or in the form of fish or some other bird or beast. Protection for the face was afforded by a lacquered mask which might be either 'somen', in which case it was a complete face, or a 'mempo' which covered only the lower half of the face. Later when the Japanese armourer came into contact with European examples he sometimes copied the style and it is possible to find an apparently European helmet made in Japan. There were numerous other forms of Japanese helmets including some which have a distinctly bizarre appearance.

Armour

A.1.   Fine spur of late 15th century, probably French—the long, slightly curved shank carried a six pointed rowel.

A.2.   Early breastplate of globose form fitted with one plate of the tace; arm pieces are separate and riveted in place. On the right is a lance rest. Late 15th century.

A.3. Half suit of Maximilian armour, close helmet with bellows visor,
breast and back plate, gorget and arm defences. The elbow guards are
unusual as the 'wings' detach. S. German c. 1510.

A.4. Maximilian breastplate with characteristic fluting, arm gussets riveted in place, the lance rest is folded back. S. German c. 1520.

A.5. LEFT: Fine gauntlet with mitten plates and roping at cuff bearing Nuremberg town stamp. A rare piece so designed that it can be locked in the 'closed' position making it almost impossible to lose the sword or mace in combat. German c. 1540. RIGHT: Tilting stirrup of 16th century fitted with several bars for the foot. Italian.

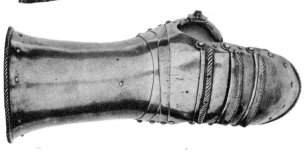

A.6. Mitten form gauntlet designed for the tilt; the cuff is larger than usual. German c. 1540.

A.7. Gothic breastplate made in two pieces and fitted with a fauld of three lames. German, late 15th century.

A.8. Maximilian close helmet of early 16th century. Spring clips secure the bevor and visor in the closed position. German.

A.9. Black and white armour with burgonet bearing the Augsburg mark; the breastplate has strong 'turn over' edges and the shoulder defences are of the spaulder type. Late 16th century.

A.10.   Black and white armour with Nuremberg mark. It has a morion
and the breastplate has the central point. The lames are detachable.

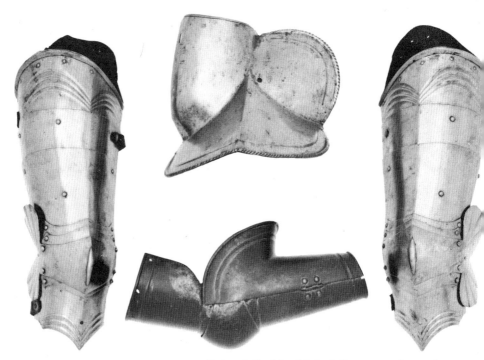

A.11. LEFT AND RIGHT: Pair of Gothic thigh defences—cuisses—late 15th century. TOP CENTRE: Extra shoulder piece—poldermitton. Third quarter of 16th century. BOTTOM CENTRE: Italian vambrace—arm defence—from a tilting armour. Third quarter of 16th century.

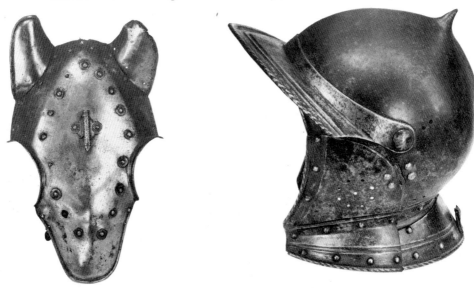

A.12. Defence for horse's head, chamfron, with ear pieces riveted on, embellished with brass headed rivets; plume holder in centre. Third quarter of 16th century.

A.13. Burgonet late 16th century—skull made from one piece—the peak pivots and ear flaps hinge at the back. German. Third quarter of 16th century.

A.14. Early 17th century, English armour for pikeman, with breastplate and wide, detachable tassets decorated with rivets and false lames.

A.16.   Half chamfron with one roped edg ear pieces riveted. Late 16th century.

A.15.   Mid-17th century burgonet—lobster pot with sliding nasal. Breastplate stamped B.P. and a crowned A.

A.17.   Breastplate with musket proof and a morion fashioned from two pieces—indication of a late date of manufacture. c. 1600.

A.18. Simple 'troopers' pot without its ear flaps. It is made from two pieces and has a one-piece neck guard with false lames. Early 17th century.

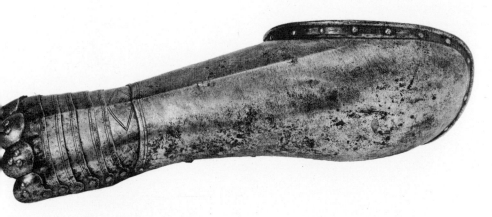

A.19. Mid-17th century elbow gauntlet for left arm. The plates to protect the fingers are missing.

A.20.   In 1813 the Russians helpe
re-equip the Prussians and supplie
some cuirasses for the Garde d
Corps. They used the cuirasses o
their Chevalier Garde with th
steel blackened.

A.21.   French cuirass of steel wit
brass overlay and chain shoulde
straps. Mid-19th century.

A.22. Officer's helmet—Bavarian Cuirassiers, c. 1825. Carries on the front the cypher of Ludwig I (1825–48). The skull is steel and the chin scale and bosses are brass.

A.23. Ceremonial helmet of German Emperor's bodyguard (Garde du Corps). The silver eagle was replaced by a fluted spike for non-parade occasions.

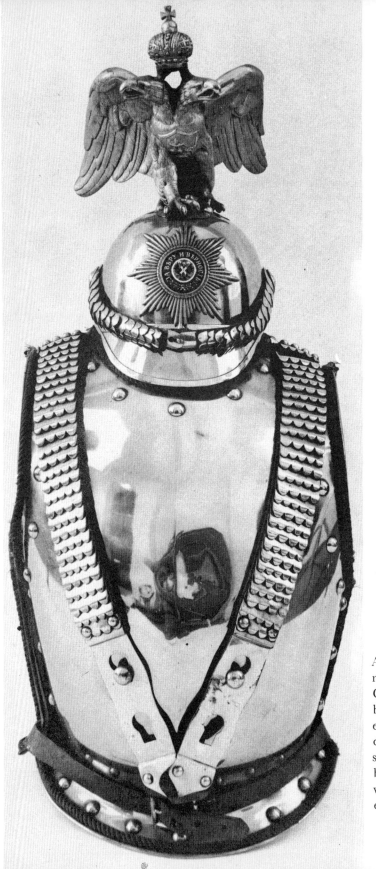

A.24. Helmet and [cui]rass of Russian Gar[de à] Cheval—the helmet [is] brass with white m[etal] edging and has a [white] double-headed eagle [with] shield on chest. [The] breastplate is brass, l[ined] with cloth and a [white] edging.

ABOVE LEFT

O.A.1.   Mameluke turban helmet decorated with silver damascening; nasal bar was originally fitted to the brow. This helmet bears the arsenal mark of St. Irene. Late 15th century.

ABOVE RIGHT

O.A.2.   Turban helmet from Persia made from a single piece of metal with three applied panels of brass and engraved. Late 15th or early 16th century.

LEFT

O.A.3.   Indo-Persian helmet with original red padded silk lining. The edge is overlaid with gilt band composed of stylised flowers with an ornate bracket to hold nasal. Late 17th or early 18th century.

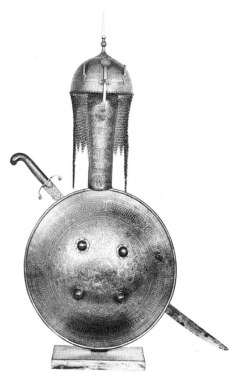

O.A.4. Items of Persian armour decorated en suite; kulah kud has usual centre spike, two plume holders and mail; the single arm guard, metal shield (dahl), and sword (shamshir) all bear etched hunting scenes. 19th century.

O.A.5. Indo-Persian kulah kud with devil's head and horns, repeated on the spike holder, single arm guard. 19th century.

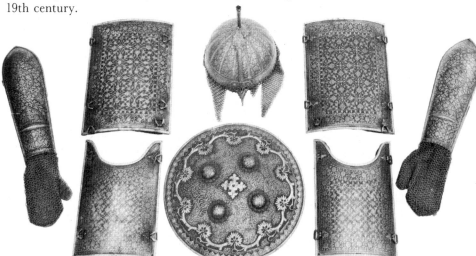

O.A.6. A suit of Mogul (Indian) armour with red velvet lining; shallow kulah kud with small mail guard. Two armguards with mail gloves; metal shield and 4 plates are main body defence.

O.A.7. Miniature Japanese armour of early 19th century with helmet
(kabuto), face mask (mempo) of russet iron, whilst cuirass (do), shoulder
guards (o-sode) and other pieces are of black lacquered iron bound with
blue silk; a copper dragon on breastplate. c. 1840.

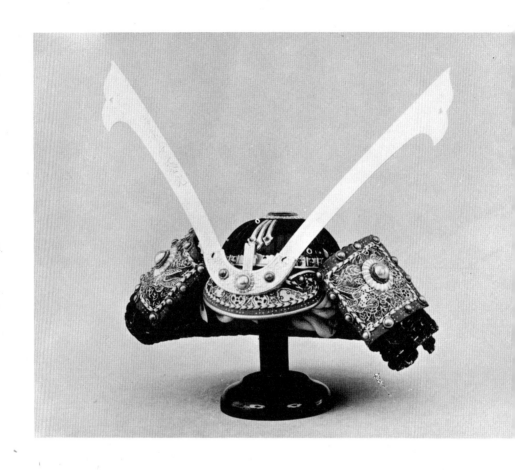

O.A.8. Miniature Japanese helmet, kabuto, made from 82 plates of black lacquered iron. Its box is marked on lid PRESENTED TO MAJOR GENERAL DRUMMOND BY PRINCE CHICHIBU IN 1928 MODEL OF A HELMET OF 14th CENTURY ARMOUR AT ITSUKUSHIMA SHRINE BY TRADITION THAT OF MINAMOTO YOSHIMITSU.

172

Collecting Arms
and Armour

For the collector of arms and armour the routine is much the same as in any other field of antiques, although there is probably less scope since many dealers rather avoid trading in weapons and armour feeling that they are, perhaps, a little too specialised. This limitation is perhaps less now than it was a few years ago when many a collector made a purchase which brightened his life simply because the antique dealer had no knowledge of the subject; nearly every collector has at least one story to tell of the old gun that turned out to be a fine wheel-lock or percussion revolver. Unfortunately, from the collector's viewpoint, this ignorance is being dispelled and the tremendous flood of books on all aspects of militaria, armour, edged weapons and firearms, has given dealers a ready source of reference. Books have also aroused more general interest in these items and this, in turn, has led to an increase in the numbers of dealers specialising in arms and armour although the total is still small in comparison with the vast number of general antique dealers. The great majority of these dealers are reliable, trustworthy people; some of whom circulate periodical lists with accurate descriptions of items for sale and so conduct a very satisfactory postal service. In addition to the dealers there are specialist auction rooms and the number of these has also increased. Some twenty years ago there were only really three sales rooms that dealt with this particular field, two in London and one in Sussex. However, many other auction houses saw the possibilities in this field and today there are at least three houses in London that hold specialised sales of arms and armour. There is one in Birmingham, one in Lewes and several others in places such as Huddersfield and Nottingham as well as many which hold occasional sales of local collections as they turn up.

In Britain one significant development over the last ten years has been the growth of the antiques fair specialising in arms and armour. In the United States Gun Shows have been a popular feature amongst collectors for many years although the quality of some was not always of the highest with displays of items that had no relevance at all to the main theme. In this country the first step was taken by the Northern Branch of the Arms and Armour Society which held its first show just outside Manchester in 1963 and, from a very small beginning the function grew in size and reputation. In 1967 the first International Arms Fair was held in London and was an instant success being repeated in subsequent years until the demand became so heavy that it is now held twice a year in early May and late September. Details of these and other shows are usually given in most antique magazines. In America most Gun Magazines list dozens of these shows each year, some very small affairs whilst others have become standing dates for the big dealers.

Another source to be explored are street markets. The proverb says that the early bird catches the worm and as far as street markets are concerned it is the early collector who catches the bargain. Most of the stall holders arrive in the very early hours of the morning and much of the main business has been completed by eight o'clock. However, street markets such as Bermondsey and Portobello Road, both in London, are so well known that it is quite likely that smaller dealers, not necessarily stall holders, who have a slightly unusual item know that they can find somebody there who will be interested and items can arrive and be "turned over", as the dealer puts it, at any time during the market's opening hours. Finally there are the advertisement columns of the newspapers and magazines and these are not to be ignored for, on occasions, it has been known for solicitors clearing up an estate or relatives saddled with, to them, unwanted items to advertise and make available items of quite outstanding interest.

The only valid advice that can usefully be given to the collector is to be persistent for whilst every collector knows the story of the windfall that drops into somebody else's unsuspecting and often undeserving lap, the majority of worthwhile items have come as a result of persistent and steady canvassing and touring and it is very important to build up connections. If a dealer knows that somebody is particularly interested in swords, the grapevine can work well. Dealers form a tight group and it is quite possible for the word to pass along the line, that so and so has a market for some particular line and he may well be offered such items.

When negotiating with a dealer one has the advantage of being there and dealing with the matter immediately but when answering adverts or bidding by post there is a lack of personal contact and no sense of immediacy and a number of extraneous matters must be considered. For the serious collector it is money well spent to invest in a subscription to the main auction houses since, for a relatively small sum, these sales rooms will send a copy, usually illustrated, of all relevant catalogues, followed, after the sale, by a price list. These catalogues usually arrive well in advance of the sale so allowing time to read them through and decide whether there is anything of interest, but here is the first snag. How accurate is the description of the weapon? Obviously there is no deliberate intent to mislead—the reputable sales room has too much to lose to falsify or in any way mislead the customer. However, the cataloguing is quite often done under pressure of a date deadline and it is quite conceivable that the cataloguers may not have the specialised knowledge to assess the finer points of some of the lots. Space is also a limiting factor since some five or six hundred lots may have to be described within a limited number of pages and this means that most items receive only a cursory description.

One of the first important things then is to assess the value of the catalogue description. This is not easy and the best hope is to attend the sales room at the viewing, when the items are put up and may be examined, and compare the items with the catalogue description. Obviously this is not always possible and many customers must rely on description for even the local purchaser may find certain difficulty in attending the viewing. Gone are those happy days when anybody could wander in and handle the various lots for nowadays security precautions have made it more than difficult for the collector to browse through the contents of a forthcoming sale. However, most reputable firms do offer a return clause in their conditions of sale so that if the customers feel that they have been badly misled and that the article is not as described, they have recourse to this clause and the lot can be returned and the money refunded.

Having examined the catalogue and decided to purchase, the next question is how best to do so. The best and most reliable method is to attend the sale personally, for then one can get the feel of the bidding and assess one's chance of success. Failing this the next best thing is to commission a dealer or friend to bid on your behalf. In the case of a professional commission agent there will obviously be some charge, the amount usually depending on the price of the item for it is normally a percentage of the total price. Whether bidding personally or being represented by an agent, it is most important to know exactly what the top bid is to be, it is fatal to follow the idea that one more bid will do it! The final result is likely to be a price that far exceeds a reasoned assessment of value. The third method is to make a postal bid and the reputable sales room will insert this bid in its correct sequence during the sale. In the past it has been known for some auction rooms to start with the figure of a postal bid but in general reliable firms do not indulge in this practice.

Having discussed the possible sources of pieces for the collection the next question is the vital one, what is any item worth? The only valid answer is that any item is worth exactly what the collector is prepared to pay, there are no set values. Auctioneers lists will tell you that at the last sale, six weeks ago, an Adam's Percussion Revolver, cased, fetched £125, but this does not mean that every cased Adam's Revolver is worth £125. The particular one in the sale may have been in good condition, it may have been a rare model, there may have been two bidders in opposition who were both anxious to obtain this item and so ran up the price. Whole hosts of factors can influence auction prices but, unfortunately, the price lists can influence dealers who, lacking any specialist knowledge, may assume that all similar items of this type are worth the amount it fetched at auction. This can be very infuriating to the collector who knows perfectly well that the item being used by the dealer as his yardstick, had some special feature. The only safe guide is to look at the item, use any figures obtained from auction lists as some guide line and then to say that, in the collector's opinion, the item is worth a certain amount. It may well be that he is prepared to go above what is considered to be the generally accepted market value but that is his privilege. Another factor which may not figure prominently in the collector's calculations, but which should nevertheless be borne in mind, is the question of appreciation. All antiques are appreciating in value and, no doubt, will continue to do so whilst in so many countries of the world inflation has depreciated the purchasing value of the currency and these two factors must be balanced. A few years ago a cased English percussion revolver could be purchased, without much difficulty, at £75, today the same model would make £125 to £150—an apparent appreciation of one hundred percent, but this figure may be more apparent than real owing to the fall in purchasing power. Nevertheless, it does mean that even if the collector may feel that he has paid rather too much, in a year or two he will almost certainly recoup his money and may, conceivably, make a profit as well.

What factors should the collector consider in trying to establish some form of relevant value? Collectors have a mixed set of standards, rarity may be the overall criterion and even if the item is in an excavated condition and practically falling to pieces, the fact that it is a very rare example of its kind may well persuade him that he must have it. Another collector may well rate rarity as being relatively less important than condition and such a collector would be very happy to purchase a moderately common example of a piece of armour or a weapon provided that it is in extremely fine condition.

Authenticity, of course, must figure prominently in the consideration of value and here the modern collector is increasingly at risk. Some 20–25 years ago the market for antique firearms, swords and armour was relatively stable and comparatively small. It was seldom worth the time and trouble of a dealer or repairer to fake items, the time and material used would hardly justify the profit realised. During the last two decades interest and demand has steadily increased until it is now unquestionably worth the restorer, or some would say the faker, increasing his output. The greatest dangers lie in the field of firearms for modern technology has made available to the restorer a wide range of hammers, frizzens, springs, lock plates, brass fittings, silver masks, indeed every component of almost any firearm. Legitimately used to restore a weapon these are perfectly acceptable but the trouble comes when after an item has changed hands two or three times, restoration has been forgotten and the item is presented as a complete and original piece. In many cases it is extremely difficult to tell the original from the replacement. Modern methods of welding and working metal have made it possible for a competent workman to conceal almost any minor flaw. The collector must settle in his own mind the question of how much restoration he is prepared to accept. Most collectors would accept that, for example, the cock of a flintlock may well be a replacement and indeed most sale catalogues point out such replacements. Whether a complete re-stock is acceptable is another matter. It is likely that most collectors would argue that it is not.

Repairs can probably be accepted but the marrying together of odd pieces to produce a complete weapon can hardly be justified on any grounds. Any antique in its original condition without replacements, restorations or alterations is obviously worth far more than a similar piece which has undergone any of these indignities and it is therefore important to recognise, as far as possible, whether the piece is in its original condition or not. There are a number of pointers, and they are little more than pointers, which can be borne in mind when examining any piece of arms and armour. With a pistol one very useful guide is the amount of pitting for almost every piece, unless it has been overcleaned and the top surface completely removed, will show some minute pits where there has been rust. In normal circumstances overall pitting should be roughly the same on all parts of the same metal. If, for example, the cock shows less or more pitting than the lock plate then there is reason to doubt that it is the original. Further guidance can be obtained by feeling the fit of the cock; does it sit firmly on the tumbler? If at all possible remove the cock and look at the square hole where it fits over the tumbler, are there any recent signs of filing? Is there any packing in order to make it fit tightly? It is unlikely that the barrel would be a complete replacement but examination of the woodwork might well indicate whether there has been recent cutting in order to get the barrel to fit comfortably. Similarly around the lock plate, are there any signs of cutting or refitting there? Has the stock a well scrubbed look? This would suggest that the pistol has been completely stripped down and possibly sanded or worked on with a polish or paint remover and then re-stained. Again, although it is appreciated that this is not always possible, if the lock can be removed and the woodwork behind it examined, this should indicate whether there has been any replacement or alteration. Decoration can also help. Is the general style of decoration the same on all the metal parts, for example cock and lock plate? It may well be that the two differ slightly; this is not conclusive proof that there has been any alteration but it might encourage a closer look at the rest.

In addition to the minutiae of the pistol there is, as most collectors would confirm, a feeling that one gets, a feeling of rightness. It may be to do with the balance, it may be to do with the shaping of the stock or the distribution of weight and although it is difficult to define most collectors would most likely agree that there is this feeling about a piece. The same general remarks apply to long arms although here repairs to the stock are likely to be a little more common owing to its greater vulnerability. Care should always be taken when examining a weapon and on no account should the hammer or the cock be allowed to fly forward on its own. After the lock has been set in the full cock position the trigger should be gently pressed whilst holding the hammer or cock so that once it has disengaged it can be allowed to come slowly back on to the nipple or frizzen. Failure to observe this simple precaution may well lead to cracked or broken nipples, hammers or cocks. The click of the engaging sear and tumbler, the feel of the main spring, all these can be guides to condition particularly when dealing with percussion. With percussion revolvers and later firearms the general condition can often be judged by the state of the blueing or browning of the barrels. The genuine heat blue of the 18th and 19th century gunmakers is of a very distinctive colour and the blueing produced by various patented pastes and liquids can never quite match the quality with the irridescent sheen that the old craftsmen produced. Any revolver which has been reblued is immediately suspect although this factor on its own, need not materially detract from its value.

When dealing with swords the question of authenticity is even more complex for, as stated above, the history of gunmakers is quite well documented but with swords one is working very largely in the dark. Little is known for instance of the regulation military pattern swords prior to the early 19th century, much may be inferred but little is known for certain, therefore it is very difficult to be dogmatic about such a sword. Again one or two guiding points can be looked at; for example, does the top of the tang, where it emerges from the pommel, show signs of having been recently filed? This would suggest that the sword has been stripped down and therefore one should be a little more careful. Does the blade sit firmly into the hilt or into the shell? Are there signs that originally a wider blade was fitted? Has the grip been replaced? Is the degree of pitting on the hilt and blade roughly the same? Another very good guide with swords is the balance; a well made sword sits comfortably in the hand and if the blade has been replaced it may be that the wrong type of blade has been used and therefore the balance has been destroyed; this feeling too becomes a second nature with the collector. It is also, of course, of vital importance to know roughly what type of blade was used with a given form of hilt; to find a double edged blade in a hilt that was normally reserved for single edged blades would obviously cause one to hesitate.

The problem, generally speaking, is less complicated when looking at armour since most reproduction armour was made by Victorians who delighted in decorating their pseudo baronial halls with fake armour. It is often of such poor quality as far as design is concerned that there is little fear of it deceiving a collector with any knowledge at all. However some very fine reproductions were made and these are more difficult to identify but there are one or two pointers. Normally the back of a plate was left rough from the hammer and a breastplate of thin metal smooth on the back, or gauntlets with no signs of working on the inner face would inevitably arouse one's doubts.

Obviously the prime aim of the collector must be knowledge and it would be a foolish person who buys without a study of the subject. The number of books on any one topic is considerable and, apart from the text, illustrations should be studied with care, preferably with a magnifying glass. Visit the museums although, in some of the smaller ones, the labels need to be treated with a certain reserve. Examine the catalogues of the large collections such as the Wallace Collection or the Tower of London. If possible make contact with other local collectors, most of whom will be only too willing to share their experiences and enjoy passing on their knowledge to a new collector. If possible visit auction rooms on view days when there is the opportunity to handle the items. All these steps are invaluable since the difference between the tyro and the expert is simply one of degree. The expert has had the opportunity to handle a multitude of items as well as having read up on his own particular topic.

It is impossible to say what should be collected for this is a personal choice which may well be conscious or just happen. Resources will obviously affect the choice since items such as inlaid wheel-locks are likely to come rather expensive and few can hope to acquire many such pieces. Many collectors start with a general acquisitive approach until suddenly one item captures their imagination and then they begin to specialise. It is important to approach collecting with a clear, unprejudiced eye for some items are "unfashionable" for no real reason and it may be that one such field, say Indian talwars, may be just the one to prove of special interest.

Assuming then that the collector has now acquired a new piece what should be the first step? Undoubtedly the greatest problem is the eternal struggle against rust. With a pistol or long arm, if it is at all feasible, one of the best assurances against damage by rust is to strip the item down completely on purchase. One very important point to bear in mind here is to use the correct size screwdriver—too large or too small a head and it may slip and score the metal. If the screws are reluctant to move then penetrating oil, gentle tapping or the old trick of heating up the screwdriver, placing it on the screw and holding it there so causing the screw to expand, may be tried. In the last resort it may be necessary to drill out the screw, but this is certainly not recommended except in desperation. Once the weapon has been stripped down and reduced to its basic components examine the pieces for rust and if there is any severe degree of rusting then it is as well to place the metal parts, brass or silver excluded, into a tray or baking tin and cover them with a mixture of paraffin and lubricating oil and leave them. If there is no danger of damaging surviving blueing or gilding, then probably the first step when dealing with severe rusting would be to go over it, not too vigorously, with a wire brush. This will remove a surprising amount of surface and even some of the deep seated rust. Having removed the greater part of the surface rust use a less coarse abrasive, following the wire brush with some steel wool, then jeweller's emery until finally one of the patent metal cleaners such as Glow can be used to give the final polish. If the barrel, or indeed any of the steelwork has been decorated with blueing or gilding and rust is present, then a difficult decision must be taken. It is not possible to remove rust and leave the gilding, blueing or browning behind, therefore it is essential to decide which is the greater importance, to retain some of the decoration or remove the rust; in general it is advisable to remove rust. One of the patent cold blueing processes can be used to touch up odd spots of damage on blued barrels but it is, at best, a poor substitute for the original. Browning is less of a problem for there are a number of well tried formulae which may be found in books such as Greener's THE GUN AND ITS DEVELOPMENT or HOME GUNSMITHING by T. Bish or THE COMPLETE GUIDE TO GUNSMITHING by C. E. Chapel and, with a degree of skill and some luck, these can produce some very attractive brown colouration.

In dealing with swords and edged weapons and armour then obviously it is not quite so easy to immerse the items in paraffin. Quite good results can be obtained by wiping the surfaces with the mixture of paraffin and oil and leaving them to stand for a day or two. After brushing the process is repeated, otherwise the procedure for removing rust is essentially the same for all pieces.

With more delicate items such as small swords, it is always worth bearing in mind that a good wash can work miracles. A good strong bath of detergent and a nail brush is always worth trying before any rust treatment is carried out and the results can often be quite astounding. There is no danger of rusting provided the article is thoroughly dried afterwards.

Once the cleaning has been carried out then some form of protection may be applied. Some collectors like to lacquer their items, and put a coat of very thin varnish over them. Unquestionably this is extremely effective, but most of these lacquers do discolour after a time and will need to be removed and replaced at some later date. More effective is perhaps the use of one of the modern silicone polishes which works remarkably well and, judiciously applied, will give a sheen and protective coat to both metal and wood. After the new acquisition has been cleaned and, if necessary, repaired or restored, and it is worth considering here whether to employ a professional if there is any delicate work to be done, the next thing is to record. This is vitally important, both for the collector's own satisfaction since a close examination of the item will often reveal features that might otherwise have been missed and also, in these unfortunate days of organised "antique" crime, it may well save him money. Some collectors prefer to make up a ring file, others use cards, some keep details listed in a book, but it is well worth recording the basic facts in some set style such as follows:

Item	Flintlock, boxlock pistol.
Date	Circa 1800.
Photograph	Yes.
Marks	London proof. Engraved H. Nock on lock plate LONDON on barrel.
Acquired	Auction—June 1971
Value	£50.
Description	Overall length............... Barrel length............ Bore...............

These entries can include all the main relevant facts and, whilst appreciating that it does involve some cost, it is worth considering the possibility of having each item photographed. If this is possible then a copy of the photograph can be attached to the card or in a separate album and appropriately numbered so that the collector has an extremely full account of each item. On the question of value, some collectors have no objection to putting the facts down in open form, others, for various reasons, prefer to keep the value of the item to themselves. In this case some code form of lettering such as used by shopkeepers is advisable. A code word or a series of numbers is chosen and the price is then transposed into the code. For example G U N H O L S T E R

1 2 3 4 5 6 7 8 9 0

£50 would therefore be £OR.

To assist in identification in the unhappy event of a theft a very small mark can be scratched somewhere out of sight and where it will do no damage—perhaps on the inside of the lock plate or the underside of a barrel.

As the collection begins to build up and increase in value it is well worth while considering the matter of insurance. Most reputable firms will insure collections although they will probably require some authentication of value from a qualified person. This may be a member of a society, or an antique dealer, who will state that, in his opinion the value of the items given is roughly correct. Again it must be borne in mind that the value of antiques appreciates annually and, therefore, it is as well to adjust the recorded value at regular intervals.

Having now cleaned, recorded, insured and perhaps photographed the item, the next step is to display. Again there are as many ways of displaying items as there are collectors and obviously much depends on the accommodation and situation of the collectors. Displaying longarms can be a problem and this may be one of the reasons why they are less popular than pistols with collectors.

They can be hung in racks affixed to the wall or stood in racks against the wall. These racks can be quite easily made from lengths of quartering with either some plastic coated hooks or else nails covered with plastic wrapping and secured to the wall. For standing racks the butt stands on the floor and the barrel rests against a batten which is cut with a series of grooves to accommodate the barrel and then secured to the wall. The longarm can be held in place by a removable bar which runs along the front of the rack.

Swords can either be displayed by hanging them from the picture rail using ordinary picture hooks and lengths of wire, or from some form of nail, again preferably covered by some form of plastic protection, driven into the wall and hooked under the hilt or grip. In the case of swords it is obviously important that they should be well secured for the dangers of a rapidly descending sword are considerable. Another point to bear in mind with all weapons on display, is that condensation in the home can be quite considerable and it is as well to check the entire collection at regular intervals so that any spots of rust may be dealt with as soon as they are detected and before they can spread and become a serious hazard. It should also be remembered that people's fingers may often be very damp with perspiration and human sweat can be extremely damaging to all metal, therefore if a piece has been handled it is worth while wiping it over with one of these silicone dusters, or oil rag, or giving it a quick polish. In the case of Japanese swords the blade should never, on any account, be touched by the bare hand, this is not only for the person's own protection, for they are usually extremely sharp, but, of even more importance is the protection of the blade for the polish on a Japanese sword blade is one of its prize attributes and to destroy that will reduce the value and interest of the sword.

Again armour presents certain of its own special problems and few collectors are lucky enough to possess a complete harness which obviously could be mounted on a dummy. It is rather more difficult when dealing with the odd piece of armour; a breast plate can be nicely hung from the wall, a gauntlet will stand on its cuff, but it is the odd leg piece or arm piece etc., that presents the problem. Probably a simple wooden frame and, for helmets, a length of broomstick fitted to a flat base is usually quite sufficient although there is an increasing use for some of these plastic wig stand heads either decorated or plain.

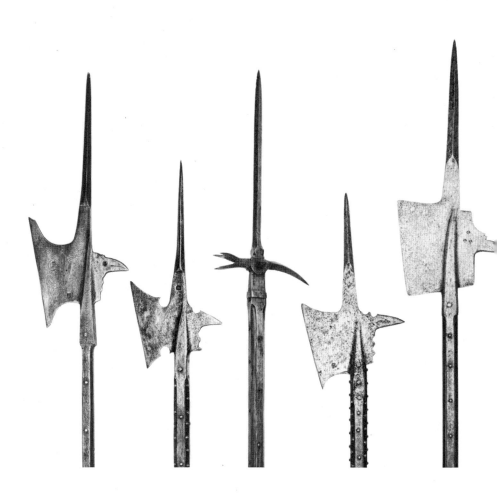

P.A.1. LEFT TO RIGHT: 1, German halberd of 16th century with long spike. 2, another with smaller head. 3, poleaxe, German 16th century. 4, heavy German halberd early 16th century. 5, halberd, early 16th century.

184

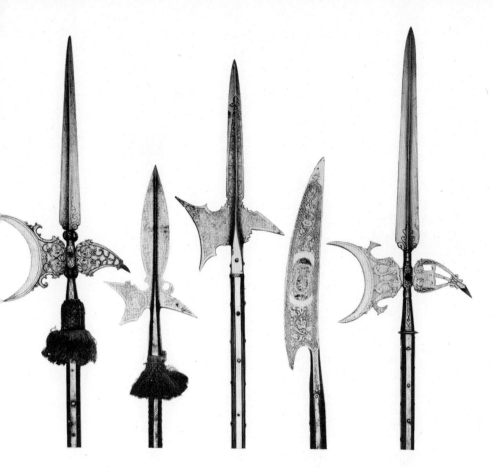

P.A.2.   LEFT to RIGHT: 1, German halberd with pierced head, first quarter of 17th century. 2, later German halberd with etched decoration. Third quarter of 17th century. 3, Austrian halberd dated 1563 on head. 4, glaive with etched arms of Archbishop of Salzburg. 5, German halberd, first quarter of 17th century with pierced head.

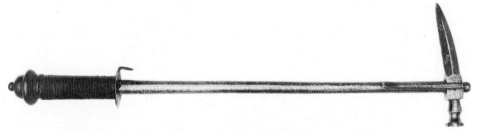

P.A.3.   War Hammer of early 17th century; these weapons were very effective for piercing armour since the spike ensured maximum impact in one small area. A hook is fitted at the top so that the weapon could hang from a wall. Length $22\frac{1}{4}$ inches. Length of head 6 inches.

185

Bibliography

Books on firearms, arms, armour, militaria, shooting and associated topics continue to flood on to the market; some are of outstanding quality, others leave a great deal to be desired. For the collector the problem is one of selection and, except for a few fortunate people, it is impossible to acquire each new one as it appears on the market; cost and limitation of space alone prevent this.

Listed below are a selection of books which, between them, pretty well cover the entire field of arms and armour for the collector. Selection has been made on the basis that the volumes should be reasonably available, in English and reliable. It is not suggested that the list is definitive, at least forty other titles of equal quality and scholarship could very easily have been added. None of the early classics, such as Hewitt's ANCIENT ARMOUR IN EUROPE, has been listed since most of them are out of print or very difficult to obtain, although the position is altering for many publishing firms are entering the reprint field and no doubt many of the classics will soon be readily available at reasonable prices. Again none of the large number of outstanding foreign language publications has been included but this is because of lack of space. Many of the books whose titles are listed will be found to give comprehensive bibliographies of such books.

In addition there are a number of periodicals which contain articles on arms and armour and these are listed below in two categories, those which are entirely devoted to relevant articles and those which contain occasional articles.

PERIODICALS DEVOTED TO ARMS AND ARMOUR AND ASSOCIATED TOPICS
Guns Review (London)
Gun Report (Aledo U.S.A.)
American Rifleman (Washington, U.S.A.)
Gun Digest (Annually; Chicago, U.S.A.)
Journal of the Arms and Armour Society (London)
Canadian Journal of Arms Collecting (Mount Royal, Canada)
Journal of the Historical Firearms Society of South Africa (Cape Town, S.A.)

PERIODICALS CONTAINING OCCASIONAL ARTICLES ON ARMS AND
ARMOUR AND ASSOCIATED TOPICS
The Connoisseur (London)
Apollo (London)
Country Life (London)
Shooting Times (London)
Collector's Guide (London)
Antique Finder (London)
Art & Antiques Weekly (London)

There are many museums which house collections of arms and
armour and for the enthusiast visits to these are essential. For details
of the collections in Britain reference should be made to
MUSEUMS AND GALLERIES IN GREAT BRITAIN AND
IRELAND published annually by Index Publishers, Dunstable,
Bedfordshire. For details of other museums throughout the world
the best publication is DIRECTORY OF MUSEUMS OF ARMS
AND MILITARY HISTORY published in Copenhagen (1970)
by the International Association of Arms and Military History.

ABELS, ROBERT   *Classic Bowie Knives* (New York 1967)
Abridgements of the Patents Specifications Relating to Firearms (London
   1960)
ALBAUGH, W.   *Confederate Handguns* (Pennsylvania 1963)
AMBER, J. T.   *Cartridges of the World* (Chicago 1969)
ANDERSON, L. J.   *Japanese Armour* (London 1968)
ANGOLIA, J.   *Swords of Hitler's Third Reich* (Essex 1969)
ANNIS, P. G.   *Naval Swords* (London 1970)
ATKINSON, J.   *Duelling Pistols* (London 1964)
ATWOOD, J.   *The Daggers and Edged Weapons of Hitler's Germany*
   (Berlin 1965)
AYLWARD, J.   *The Small Sword in England* (London 1960)
BAILEY, D. W.   *British Military Longarms 1715–1815* (London 1971)
BAXTER, D.   *Blunderbusses* (London 1970)
BAXTER, D. R.   *Superimposed Load Firearms 1360–1860* (Hong Kong
   1966)
BISH, T.   *Home Gunsmithing Digest* (Chicago 1970)
BLACKMORE, H. L.   *Arms and Armour* (London and New York 1965)
BLACKMORE, H. L.   *British Military Firearms* (London 1961)
BLACKMORE, H. L.   *Firearms* (London 1964)
BLACKMORE, H. L.   *Guns and Rifles of the World* (London 1968)
BLACKMORE, H. L.   *Hunting Weapons* (London 1972)

BLAIR, C.   *European and American Arms 1100–1850* (London 1962)

BLAIR, C.   *European Armour* (London 1958)

BLAIR, C.   *Pistols of the World* (London 1968)

BOOTHROYD, G.   *The Handgun* (London 1970)

CAREY, A. M.   *English, Irish and Scottish Firearms Makers* (Reprinted London 1960)

CARTER, J. A.   *Allied Bayonets of World War II* (London 1969)

CHAPEL, C. E.   *The Complete Guide to Gunsmithing* (New York 1962)

COGGINS, J.   *Arms and Equipment of the Civil War* (New York 1962)

DARLING, A. D.   *Red Coat and Brown Bess* (Ottawa 1970)

DAVIDSON, H. R.   *The Sword in Anglo-Saxon England* (Oxford 1962)

DIXON, N.   *Georgian Pistols 1715–1840* (London 1972)

DOWELL, W. C.   *The Webley Story* (Leeds 1962)

DUNLAP, J.   *American, British and Continental Pepperbox Firearms* (1967)

GARDNER, R.   *Small Arms Makers* (New York 1953)

GEORGE, J. N.   *English Guns and Rifles* (Plantersville, South Carolina 1947)

GEORGE, J. N.   *English Pistols and Revolvers* (London Reprint 1963)

GREENER, W. W.   *The Gun and its Development*, 9th Edition (London 1910) (Reprint London 1972)

HANSON, C.   *The Plains Rifle* (New York 1960)

HAWYARD, J.   *The Art of the Gunmaker* Vol. I (London 1965) Vol. II (London 1963)

HELD, R.   *The Age of Firearms* (London 1959). Revised edition (Northfield, Illinois 1970)

HICKS, J. E.   *French Military Weapons* (Connecticut 1964)

HOGG, I. V.   *German Pistols and Revolvers 1871–1945* (London 1971)

JACKSON, H. T. and WHITELAW, C.   *European Hand Firearms* (Reprint New York, N.D.)

KARR, C. L. and C. R.   *Remington Handguns* (New York 1960)

KAUFFMAN, H.   *Early American Gunsmiths* (New York 1952)

KAUFFMAN, H.   *The Pennsylvania-Kentucky Rifle* (Harrisburg, Penn. 1960)

KNUTSEN, R.   *Japanese Polearms* (London 1963)

LAVIN, J. D.   *A History of Spanish Firearms* (London 1965)

LENK, T.   *The Flintlock* (London reprint 1965)

LOGAN, H.   *Underhammer Guns* (Harrisburg, Pennsylvania 1960)

LORD, F. A.   *Civil War Collectors Encyclopaedia* (Harrisburg, Pennsylvania 1965)

MAY, W. E. and ANNIS, P. G. W.   *Swords for Sea Service* (London 1970)

MOLLO, A.   *Daggers of the Third German Reich* (London 1967)

MOLLO, E.   *Russian Military Swords 1801–1917* (London 1969)

NEAL, W. K. and BACK, D. H.   *Forsyth & Co. Patent Gunmakers* (London 1969)

NEAL, W. K. and BACK, D. H.   *The Mantons Gunmakers* (London 1967)

NEAL, R. J. and JINKS, R. G.   *Smith and Wesson 1857–1945* (London and New York 1966)

NEUMANN, G.   *The History of Weapons of the American Revolution* (New York and London 1967)

NORMAN, V.   *Arms and Armour* (London 1964)

NORMAN, A. V.   *Small-Swords and Military Swords* (London 1967)

NORMAN, A. V. and POTTINGER, D.   *Warrior to Soldier* (London 1966)

NUTTER, W. E.   *Manhattan Firearms* (Harrisburg 1958)

OAKESHOTT, R. E.   *The Archaeology of Weapons* (London 1960)

OAKESHOTT, R. E.   *The Sword in the Age of Chivalry* (London 1964)

PARTINGTON, J. R.   *A History of Greek Fire and Gunpowder* (Cambridge 1960)

PETERSON, H. L.   *American Knives* (New York 1958)

PETERSON, H. L.   *American Silver Mounted Swords 1700–1815* (New York 1955)

PETERSON, H. L.   *Arms and Armour in Colonial America* (America 1956)

PETERSON, H. L.   *Daggers and Fighting Knives of the Western World* (London 1968)

PETERSON, H. L.   *Encyclopaedia of Firearms* (London 1964)

RAWSON, P. S.   *The Indian Sword* (London 1968)

RILING, R   *Guns and Shooting* (New York 1951)

RILING, R.   *The Powder Flask Book* (New Hope, Pennsylvania 1953)

ROADS, C. H.   *The British Soldier's Firearm 1850–1864* (London 1964)

ROBINSON, B. W.   *Arts of the Japanese Sword* (London 1961)

ROBINSON, H. R.   *Japanese Arms and Armour* (London 1969)

ROBINSON, H. R.   *Oriental Armour* (London 1967)

SNODGRASS, A.   *Arms and Armour of the Greeks* (London 1967)

STEPHENS, F.   *Collectors Pictorial Book of Bayonets* (London 1971)

STONE, G. C.   *A Glossary of Construction, Decoration and use of Arms and Armour* (Reprinted 1966)

SUTHERLAND, R. G. and WILSON, R. L.   *The Book of Colt Firearms* (Kansas City 1971)

SWAYZE, N. L.   *'51 Colt Navies* (Yazoo City, Mississipi 1967)

TAYLERSON, A.   *Revolving Arms* (London 1967)

TAYLERSON, A., ANDREWS, R. and FRITH, J.   *The Revolver 1818–1865* (London 1968)

TAYLERSON, A.   *The Revolver 1865–1888* (London 1966)

TAYLERSON, A. W.   *The Revolver 1889–1914* (London 1970)

WAGNER, E.   *Cut and Thrust Weapons* (London 1967)

Wallace Collection Catalogues (London, various)

WALLACE, J.   *Scottish Swords and Dirks* (London 1970)

WATSON, G.   *The Roman Soldier* (London 1969)

WEBSTER, G.   *The Roman Imperial Army* (London 1969)

WILKINSON, F.   *Arms and Armour* (London 1971)

WILKINSON, F.   *Battle Dress* (London 1970)

WILKINSON, F.   *British and American Flintlocks* (London 1971)

WILKINSIN, F.   *Edged Weapons* (London 1970)

WILKINSON, F.   *Flintlock Guns and Rifles* (London   )

WILKINSON, F.   *Flintlock Pistols* (London 1968)

WILKINSON, F.   *Guns* (London 1970)

WILKINSON, F.   *Small Arms* (London 1966)

WILKINSON, F.   *Swords and Daggers* (London 1967)

WILKINSON, F.   *Antique Firearms* (London 1969)

WILLIAMSON, H.   *Winchester—The Gun That Won the West* (London & New York 1963)

WINANT, L.   *Early Percussion Firearms* (London 1961)

WINANT, L.   *Firearms Curiosa* (London 1956)